MODERN HUMANS

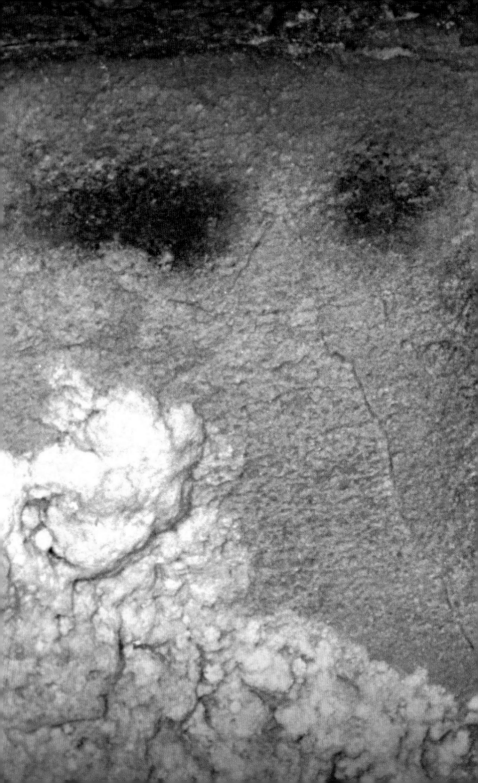

HUMANS: AN EVOLUTIONARY HISTORY

MODERN HUMANS

REBECCA STEFOFF

Marshall Cavendish
Benchmark

Marshall Cavendish Benchmark
99 White Plains Road
Tarrytown, New York 10591
www.marshallcavendish.us

LIBRARY OF CONGRESS CATALOGING-IN-PUBLICATION DATA
Stefoff, Rebecca   Modern humans / by Rebecca Stefoff.   p. cm. —   (Humans : an evolutionary history)
Includes bibliographical references and index.   Summary: "Describes the rise of modern humans, *Homo sapiens*,
including the theories about our origins and how we spread throughout the world, with information
based on the latest fossil and DNA studies"—Provided by publisher.   ISBN 978-0-7614-4187-8
1. Human beings—Origin. 2. Human evolution. 3. Human population genetics. 4. Paleoanthropology.
I. Title.   GN281S783 2010   569.9—dc22   2009012364

Editor: Joyce Stanton   Publisher: Michelle Bisson   Art Director: Anahid Hamparian
Series Designer: Meghan Dewar/MichaelNelsonDesign   Drawings, charts, and maps by Robert Romagnoli

Images provided by Debbie Needleman, Picture Researcher, Portsmouth, NH, from the following sources: *Front Cover:* ©Philippe
Plailly & Atelier Daynes/Photo Researchers, Inc. *Back Cover:* Bison from the Caves at Altamira. Santilla del Mar, Cantabria,
Spain/©The Bridgeman Art Library. *Pages i, 70 (right):* Réunion des Musées Nationaux /Art Resource, NY.; *pages ii-iii:* ©Ancient
Art & Architecture Collection Ltd.; *pages vi (top), 20:* ©Volker Steger/Science Photo Library/Photo Researchers, Inc.; *pages vi
(second from top), 36:* ©James King-Holmes/Photo Researchers, Inc.; *pages vi (third from top), 60:* ©Philippe Plailly & Atelier
Daynes/Photo Researchers, Inc.; *pages vi (fourth from top), 70 (left), 71:* ©Erich Lessing/Art Resource, NY.; *pages vi (fifth from top),
76:* ©John Stanmeyer/VII/Associated Press; *pages vi (bottom), 87:* Library of Congress, Prints & Photographs Division, Edward
S. Curtis Collection, Reproduction Number: LC-USZ62-46892; *page vii (top):* Bison from the Caves at Altamira. Santilla del Mar,
Cantabria, Spain/©The Bridgeman Art Library; *pages vii (bottom), 44, 45:* ©Biophoto Associates/Photo Researchers, Inc.; *page 8:*
©Andreas Feininger/Time & Life Pictures/Getty Images; *page 10:* ©Richard Lewis/Associated Press; *page 13:* ©Mary
Altaffer/Associated Press; *page 14:* ©The Print Collector/Alamy; *page 16:* ©John Collier/The Bridgeman Art Library/Getty
Images; *page 18:* ©Alison Jones/DanitaDelimont.com; *page 21:* ©Drew/Trace Images/The Image Works; *page 22:* ©Kenneth
Garrett/National Geographic/Getty Images; *pages 23, 29, 95 (top):* Photo ©akg-images, London/Hess. Landesmuseum; *page 24:*
©Private Collection/The Bridgeman Art Library/Getty Images; *page 27:* ©Robert Harding Picture Library Ltd/Alamy; *page 32:*
©Bill Sanderson/Photo Researchers, Inc.; *pages 37, 94:* ©Gary Carlson/Photo Researchers, Inc.; *page 41:* Courtesy of Rebecca
L. Cann; *page 46:* ©The Natural History Museum/Alamy; *page 51:* ©Photo by Joe Angeles/WUSTL photo; *page 57:* ©Ira
Block/National Geographic/Getty Images; *page 59:* ©Gianni Dagli Orti/CORBIS; *page 62 (left):* KENNETH GARRETT/National
Geographic Image Collection; *page 62 (right):* ©The Natural History Museum, London; *page 64:* Courtesy of the French Min-
istry of Culture and Communication, Regional Direction for Cultural Affairs - Rhône-Alpes region - Regional Department of
Archaeology; *page 66:* ©AFP/DIRECTION REGIONALE DES AFFAIRES CULTURELLES/Getty Images; *pages 68-69:* ©Peter V.
Bianchi/National Geographic/Getty Images; *page 73:* ©ANNA ZIEMINSKI/AFP/Getty Images; *page 74:* IRA BLOCK/National
Geographic Image Collection; *page 78:* ©AFP PHOTO/NATURE/HO/MJ MORWOOD/Getty Images; *page 79:* Image courtesy
of Kirk E. Smith, Mallinckrodt Institute of Radiology, Washington University School of Medicine, St. Louis, MO.; *page 80:*
STEPHEN ALVAREZ/National Geographic Image Collection; *page 81:* ©MICHAEL NICHOLS/National Geographic Image Col-
lection; *pages 82, 95 (bottom):* ©Mission archéologique de Qafzeh/Photo Researchers, Inc.; *page 90:* ©Jeff Barnard/Associated
Press; *page 91:* ©Jane Ades/NHGRI; *page 92:* ©YOSHIKAZU TSUNO/AFP/Getty Images.

Printed in Malaysia
135642

Front cover: *A reconstruction of a Cro-Magnon man, one of the first modern humans in Europe*
Half-title page: *Carved from mammoth ivory, this figure, known as the Lady with the Hood, is about
23,000 years old. Although it appears large, it is tiny—less than two inches tall.*
Title page: *A hand print, one form of ancient cave art*
Back cover: *A bison, one of the many prehistoric creatures painted on cave walls at Altamira, Spain*

With special thanks

to Rob DeSalle, Curator, Sackler Institute for Comparative Genomics,

American Museum of Natural History, New York,

for his valuable comments and careful reading of the manuscript.

CONTENTS

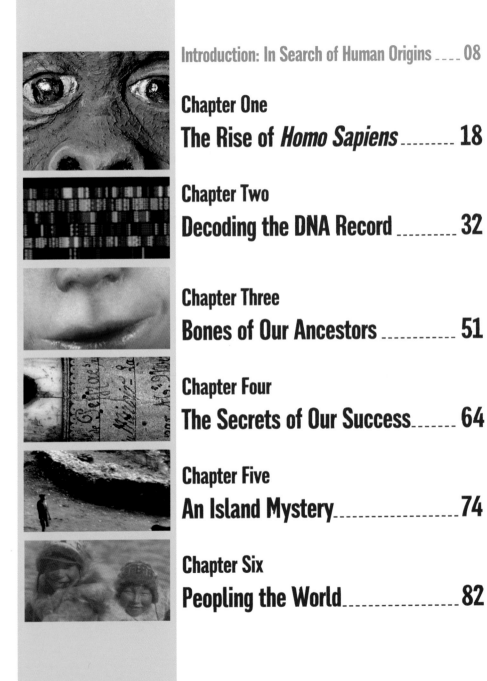

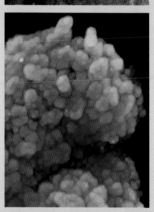

In Search of Human Origins

It was the completion of a scientific venture as momentous as the race to split the atom or the mission to land on the Moon.

The adventure had begun in an English laboratory, where a team of researchers studied life at the level of individual cells. James Watson, Francis Crick, Maurice Wilkins, and Rosalind Franklin made scientific history in 1953 when they discovered the structure of DNA, the material inside each cell that is the blueprint for every species of plant and animal. That discovery launched a revolution in genetics, the scientific exploration of how DNA carries information from one generation to the next and gives life its form.

Four years after helping to discover the structure of DNA, James Watson showed how its molecules are arranged in a spiral form called a double helix.

Half a century later, in what Watson called "a truly momentous occasion for every human being around the globe," another team of researchers announced another triumph.[1] The Human Genome Project had been completed. For years, scientists from many different countries had been working on decoding and mapping the DNA of

Homo sapiens, the species to which all living people belong. The completion of that project was announced on April 14, 2003. The combined efforts of hundreds of people had brought humankind's understanding of itself to a new milestone. For the first time, more than 99 percent of the human genome, the arrangement of DNA that is unique to our species, was known.

An Adventure into Ourselves

"The Human Genome Project has been an amazing adventure into ourselves, to understand our own DNA instruction book, the shared inheritance of all humankind," said Francis Collins, the director of the American part of the project, on the day of the announcement.[2] Medical researchers greeted the new map of the human genome with excitement, knowing that it would help them understand the causes of some diseases, which might lead to cures. Also taking a keen interest in the Human Genome Project—and in a parallel study of the human genome by a private company—was the international community of paleoanthropologists, the scientists who study human origins. To paleoanthropologists, our genome is more than a blueprint. It is also a coded history of our species, from its distant origins to the present day.

In April 2003 the scientific journal *Nature* published a special issue about the completion of the Human Genome Project.[3] Less than two months later, more news about human origins appeared in *Nature*. Scientists had determined that three fossil skulls from Ethiopia belonged to members of our species who lived around 160,000 years ago. These skulls had been found in 1997 at a place called Herto. Now, six years later, they were recognized as the oldest-known traces of *Homo sapiens*.[4]

Genes and bones are our main sources of information about how the human species developed over time. The genome map and the Herto fossils gave paleoanthropologists a wealth of new evidence. But the year 2003 brought still more excitement. In September a team of researchers made an astonishing discovery in a cave on Flores Island, in the Southeast Asian nation of Indonesia. While looking for evidence of early human settlement on the island, the researchers unearthed the bones of adult humans who had been only about three feet (one meter) tall. These remains soon gained the nickname "hobbits," after the small beings in J. R. R. Tolkien's fantasy tales *The Hobbit* and *The Lord of the Rings*.

British paleoanthropologist Chris Stringer marvels at a cast made from the small skull of one of the Flores Island "hobbits."

The exceptionally small Flores people were completely unknown to science. The discovery of their remains kicked off a debate among paleoanthropologists, biologists, and medical experts that continues to this day. Some argue that the bones came from members of our species, reduced to tiny size by disease or deformity. Other experts— including the discoverers of the bones—claim that the Flores hobbits were an entirely different species, *Homo floresiensis*. If this view proves to be correct, the most remarkable thing about *H. floresiensis* will not be its tiny size. The most remarkable thing will be the fact that these little people were alive very recently, compared with other extinct human species such as the Neanderthals. *Homo floresiensis* may not have become extinct until just 13,000 years ago, after *H. sapiens* had colonized the same part of the world.[5]

The find on Flores shook up much of what scientists thought they knew about the recent history of the hominins, the group that includes humans and their now-extinct relatives. One scientific article declared that the Flores fossils were "among the most outstanding discoveries in paleoanthropology for half a century."[6] Experts are still debating the meaning of the fossils, which may revise the story of the human past.

Like the human genome sequence and the Herto skulls, the surprising find on Flores gave scientists new clues in the search for knowledge about human origins. Together with many other discoveries and insights, these pieces of evidence help us better understand the place of our species, *Homo sapiens*, in the long history of human evolution.

Darwin's Big Idea

To understand human evolution, we must know something about evolution in general. Evolution is the pattern of biological change over time as new species appear and old ones die out. The basic unit of evolution is not the individual organism, or living thing. Instead, evolution occurs at the level of species, or types of living thing.

Biologists admit that *species* is a somewhat slippery term to define, and they have taken a variety of approaches to the definition. For many years, one of the most widespread definitions said that a species is a group of plants or animals that are reproductively isolated from other organisms. Reproductive isolation does not mean that the plants or animals are stranded on a desert island, lonely and unable to find mates. It means that under natural conditions the plants or animals within the species reproduce with each other but not with organisms outside the species. One problem with this definition is that it does not apply to organisms such as bacteria that can reproduce on their own, without partners.

In recent years, as researchers have decoded the genomes of an ever-growing number of organisms, many scientists have added a genetic element to their definition of *species*. They now call a species a group of organisms that share the same genome and, if they reproduce sexually, do so only with other organisms in the group. A species may be distributed over a wide or even a worldwide range, like modern humans, or it may occupy a range as small as a single tree, like some rain-forest insects.

Since ancient times people have grouped plants and animals into species, but they thought that species were permanent and unchanging. Life on Earth, in other words, had always been the same. By the nineteenth century, however, new scientific insights were challenging that view. Geology had shown that Earth is far older than people once believed; we now know that the age of our planet is measured in billions, not thousands, of years. Naturalists, people who studied the natural world, had examined fossils of dinosaurs and other creatures that no longer existed, and they had realized that many kinds of life had become extinct. If species could disappear into extinction, some naturalists asked, could they also appear? Had new species come on the scene during the long history of life?

The answer to that question came from a British naturalist named Charles Darwin. Although a number of naturalists were exploring the question of species at around the same time, Darwin was the first to reach a wide audience. After pondering and testing his ideas for more than twenty years, in 1859 Darwin published *On the Origin of Species*, a book that he called "one long argument" in support of his central claim.[7] That claim was that species change over time, and that new species develop from existing ones. At first Darwin did not use the word *evolution* to refer to this ongoing pattern. He called it "descent with modification." The term *evolution* appeared in the fifth edition of *Origin* in 1869, however, and ever since then it has been linked to Darwin.

New species evolved, Darwin explained, through a process that he

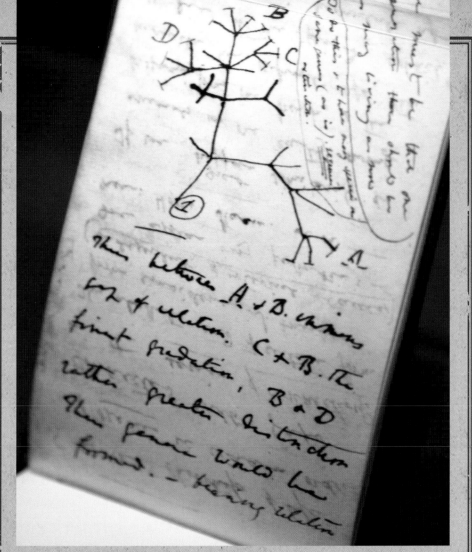

In his journal Charles Darwin sketched a "tree of life" showing evolutionary relationships. It reflects his insight that new species are formed from existing ones.

called natural selection. He pointed out that humans have created many breeds, or varieties, of domesticated animals and plants through artificial selection, by choosing plants or animals that have desirable qualities and breeding them with each other. Artificial selection has enabled people to mold dogs, for example, into varieties that range from huge, hairy sheepdogs to tiny, bald Chihuahuas. Something similar occurs in the natural world, Darwin argued. Over long periods of time, natural selection creates not just new varieties within species but distinct new species.

Fancy pigeon breeds, as Darwin pointed out, are created by artificial selection.

It works like this: Organisms pass on their characteristics to their offspring, but the characteristics inherited by the offspring include random, natural changes known as variations, or mutations. If the mutations help an organism's offspring—or, at least, do not harm them—then the offspring will survive to reproduce, passing on their characteristics, including the new features, to their own offspring. In time, as individuals possessing the new features reproduce with each other, those features will be reinforced as they spread through the population. At some point the organisms that evolved with the new features will be different enough from the original organisms to be considered a new species.

Natural selection explained how evolution could take place. In the struggle to survive, Darwin claimed, some organisms inherited favorable variations that gave them advantages in their particular environments or ways of life. Those organisms could then outcompete other organisms that belonged to the same species but lacked the favorable new variations. A bird with a slightly longer beak, for example, would be able to pluck insects from deeper cracks in logs and tree trunks than the other birds could manage. This would give the longer-beaked bird an edge in survival.

Yet Darwin could not explain the mechanism of heredity—exactly how parents transmitted characteristics to their children, and how variations occurred in those characteristics. Not until the science of genetics developed in the twentieth century, bringing important discoveries about the roles of genes and DNA, did scientists grasp the mechanisms of genetic inheritance and genetic variation.

Work in Progress

Near the end of *On the Origin of Species*, Darwin wrote that when the world came to accept his findings there would be "a considerable revolution in natural history."[8] An understanding of evolution, he said, would not only enrich the sciences but would give people a whole new view of life—all forms of life. "Light," Darwin predicted, "will be thrown on the origin of man and his history."[9]

On the Origin of Species is not a short book (although it is a lot shorter than Darwin initially meant it to be). Yet that single sentence near the end of the book is Darwin's only mention of human origins. Darwin was well aware that many people would be disturbed by the idea that plant and animal species changed and evolved naturally, rather than receiving their complete and final forms through divine creation. Even some of those who could accept the evolution of plants and animals might reject the idea that human beings, too, were part of this natural process. Placing humans in the natural order would seem to go against religious traditions.

Although Darwin devoted just one sentence in *On the Origin of Species* to human origins, his readers had no trouble making the connection between evolution and humankind. Many of them, as he had expected, were outraged. They were disgusted by the suggestion that humans had evolved from animals, and they found the possibility that human origins were natural rather than supernatural to be irreligious. Others, convinced by Darwin's mass of evidence, accepted the reality of evolution in the natural world. Many of these readers recognized that

Darwin's passion for knowledge led him to the study of such organisms as earthworms and orchids.

evolution applies to humans just as it applies to other forms of life, and they were able to reconcile the new concept with their religious beliefs. In 1871 Darwin tackled the ticklish subject of people and evolution head-on in a book called *The Descent of Man.* It was one of the early steps in an investigation of human origins that is still going on today.

Although the fact of evolution is now established beyond reasonable scientific doubt, much remains to be learned about how it occurs. As part of the scientific process, experts constantly examine new evidence. This frequently leads them to revise or fine-tune their ideas about the mechanisms of evolution and also about the rate at which speciation, or the emergence of new species, takes place. Evolutionary scientists now know that natural selection is not the only factor that influences the development of new species. Climate change, new mutations, movements of populations, inbreeding, and random chance also play a role in speciation. One lively area of modern evolutionary research, for example, is population genetics, which studies the different ways that genetic variations occur and spread in populations of different sizes, including human populations.

"The proper study of mankind is man," wrote the British poet Alexander Pope in the 1730s.[10] People of all times and cultures have speculated about the nature and origins of humankind. In the modern world, science has allowed us to probe deeply into our own nature, yet where we came from and how we came to be what we are today remains a complicated puzzle. More pieces of the puzzle are missing than have been found, but each new discovery adds to the picture, even if the experts are not yet certain where it fits.

For this work in progress, scientists use what has been called "a toolbox for human origins."[11] The tools in the toolbox are an array of techniques and skills that fall into three broad categories. One category is genetics, the study of how DNA and genes work. Another is paleoanthropology, which studies ancient human life through physical traces such as fossils and stone tools. The third category is evolutionary science, which looks at the big picture of evolution, with topics such as population genetics and natural selection.

Modern people—Homo sapiens, to scientists—are the only members of the human family that exist today. Yet during the past century and a half, scientists have learned that over the span of millions of years, evolution has produced many other species of humans or close human relatives, all of which are now extinct. In the years since the publication of On the Origin of Species, hundreds of scientific discoveries have thrown light, just as Darwin predicted, on human evolution.

The first book in this series, Origins, told of the search for the earliest human ancestors and the discovery of the australopiths, a branch of the family tree that flourished in Africa several million years ago. The second book, First Humans, focused on other branches of the family tree, including the first true humans, members of the genus Homo. The third book, Ice Age Neanderthals, introduced several human species that lived in Eurasia during the Ice Age. This book, Modern Humans, looks at the origins of Homo sapiens and how our species spread throughout the world. The four books together tell the story of human evolution as it is known today.

As she gazes across the Omo River in Ethiopia, this woman surveys humankind's heartland. Many important human fossils—from earlier species as well as our own—have come to light here.

ONE

The Rise of *Homo sapiens*

Since Charles Darwin's time, science has made great steps toward solving the mystery of human origins. We know, for example, that modern humans are the most recent chapter in a long history of human evolution, and that they evolved from ancestors that are now extinct. But when did our species come into existence? Where did we originate, and how did we become what we are today?

Hominins, Humans, and *Homo sapiens*

In the late nineteenth century, Darwin made two claims about human origins. First, he said that the people and apes of the modern world are descended from the same long-ago ancestors. Second, he claimed that the human lineage—the line of evolutionary descent leading to humans— originated in Africa. Scientists would discover that Darwin was right on both counts.

Humans belong to the primate order, a subgroup of mammals that also includes apes, monkeys, and a variety of other creatures such as lemurs. Our closest living relatives within the primate order are the African apes, particularly chimpanzees. Our lineage and their lineage, however, separated between 7 million and 5 million years ago, long before the modern apes came into existence. The species that evolved in the human lineage after that split—including our species—are the hominins.

All known fossils of early hominins have been found in Africa. There, by at least 4 million years ago, appeared the first species in a group called the australopiths. These hominins more closely resembled apes than humans,

The australopiths of East Africa probably looked much like this museum model.

and their brains were not much larger than those of modern chimpanzees. Yet the australopiths had one important human trait. They were bipeds, meaning that they walked upright on two legs, rather than on four legs like other primates. (For more information about the beginnings of the human line and the australopiths, see *Origins*, the first book in this series.)

By about 2.5 million years ago, a second key human trait had appeared. Hominins had become toolmakers, shaping small stones into simple cutting tools by hammering them with other stones. At that time Africa was home to several kinds of hominins, and paleoanthropologists do not know for certain which of them made the first tools. By 2 million years ago, however, new toolmakers had evolved in Africa. These are the first hominins that scientists consider human—members of the genus *Homo*, the subgroup of hominins that includes our own species.

The most widespread of the early *Homo* species was *Homo erectus*. This long-lasting and successful species was more humanlike than the australopiths, although its bony, ridged forehead and lack of a chin gave it an appearance unlike our own. And although *H. erectus*'s brain was smaller than ours, it was significantly larger than that of the australopiths. The hominin line was developing greater brainpower.

Some of our earliest human ancestors migrated out of Africa thousands of years ago. Homo sapiens evolved later, probably in Africa, the home of modern populations such as the San people of the Kalahari Desert.

In addition to creating larger, more complex stone tools than had been known before, *H. erectus* extended its range over more of the world than any earlier hominin. As groups or families of this species traveled in search of food or new territory, some of them left the continent in which they had originated. They migrated out of Africa, crossing the Sinai Peninsula from what is now Egypt into western Asia. Paleoanthropologists sometimes call this migration Out of Africa I (or OOAI).[12]

In 1991 the remains of ancient hominins turned up in a town called Dmanisi in the nation of Georgia, on the border between Europe and Asia. Experts estimate that the fossils date from about 1.8 million years ago, during a period of Earth's history that geologists call the Pleistocene epoch. Up to the time of the Dmanisi discovery, the only hominin remains of that age found in Eurasia belonged to *Homo erectus*. The Dmanisi fossils appeared different, however. They had smaller brains than the known *H. erectus* fossils. Paleoanthropologists have not yet decided whether the

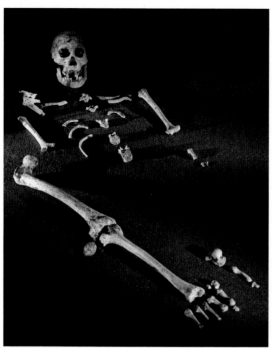
Skeletal remains from Dmanisi, Georgia, show that humans had reached Eurasia long before modern Homo sapiens *existed.*

Dmanisi fossils belong to *H. erectus*, to a hybrid or transitional form, or to some other, possibly unknown type of early hominin. The fossils prove, though, that hominins were living in Eurasia nearly 2 million years ago.

Farther east, fossil remains from the Indonesian island of Java show that *Homo erectus* had reached Southeast Asia by fairly early in the Pleistocene, around 1.5 million years ago. The species also became established in China. Some paleoanthropologists think that these Asian populations had evolved far enough away from their African ancestors to be considered a separate species. Those who share this view call the parent species in Africa *Homo ergaster* and the Asian species *Homo erectus*. The Indonesian variety of *H. erectus* has also been called Java Man, while Chinese *H. erectus* became known as Peking Man, because English-speaking people once used that name for Beijing, the Chinese capital. (See *First Humans*, the second book in this series, for more information on the early species of *Homo* and the fossil finds in Georgia, Java, and China.)

Homo erectus continued to live in Asia for hundreds of thousands of years, long after the species became extinct in Africa. Other types of early humans, meanwhile, had evolved in Africa. By around a million years ago, some of them had ventured into Europe, although only a few traces of these early migrants have been found, and scientists are not certain of their species.

Reconstructions of eight human species, including Homo erectus *(front left) and Neanderthal Man (back left). All are now extinct.*

Fossils show that a different kind of human had become established in Africa by about 640,000 years ago and in Europe by at least 500,000 years ago, during the middle of the Pleistocene epoch. These people had larger brains than *Homo erectus*, and their skulls were less bony. Many paleoan-thropologists group these fossils together under the name *Homo heidelber-gensis*, or Heidelberg Man, after a jawbone found in Germany. Other experts think that the so-called Heidelberg Man fossils represent more than one species.

In Europe, Heidelberg Man was eventually replaced by *H. nean-derthalensis*, or Neanderthal Man. This large-brained human lived in Europe starting about 175,000 years ago and also occupied many sites in western Asia. (*Ice Age Neanderthals*, the third book in this series, tells the story of these early humans.) *H. erectus*, meanwhile, continued to live far-ther east in Asia.

Based on fossil finds, paleoanthropologists think that *Homo erectus* became extinct in China about 250,000 years ago. This early human survived longer on the island of Java. Fossils found there at a place called Ngangdong have traditionally been dated to about 100,000 years ago, although one study suggests that they may be only half that age, some 50,000 years old.[13] The Neanderthals disappeared even more recently, slipping into extinction less than 30,000 years ago.

By the time the Neanderthals became extinct, a new kind of human had spread across Africa, Europe, and much of Asia. These new people had even made their way across the sea to Australia. The human species that flourished after the others disappeared, and that continues to flourish today, is *Homo sapiens*.

Questions about Recent Human Evolution

Every time someone discovers a new hominin fossil, scientists learn more about one of the species on our family tree. The connections between species, though, are not always clear. When scientists draw diagrams of the evolutionary links between hominin species or groups of species, they set up hypotheses, or ideas about possible relationships, and then test, study, and criticize each one.

One artist's vision of a Neanderthal. Experts think these large-brained humans differed in many ways from our own species.

Paleoanthropologists do not know for certain, for example, that the genus *Homo* evolved from one of the species in the australopith group, but that interpretation fits the evidence. No better candidate for an ancestor to *Homo* has been found in the fossil record. Even within the *Homo* genus, closer to the present, scientists cannot trace the links between species with absolute certainty. The Neanderthals are a good example. Many experts think that *Homo neanderthalensis* evolved from European populations of *H. heidelbergensis*. However, some think that Heidelberg Man and Neanderthal Man, along with *H. erectus*, evolved from African *H. ergaster*.

What about *Homo sapiens*? How do we fit into the picture, and which of these extinct species of humans was our immediate ancestor? To answer those questions, scientists have proposed several theories, or models, of how humans evolved over the past 2 million years. Two theories, the multi-regional model and the out-of-Africa model, have competed for scientific support since the 1980s. In recent years, some researchers have presented compromise models that combine features from both of these theories.

The Multiregional Model

After people in the late nineteenth and early twentieth centuries started finding fossils that were identified as extinct human species, scientists started wondering about the relationship between those extinct species and modern humans. Some of their theories focused on racial differences.

In the nineteenth century, some European scholars held the notion that the different races, or varieties, of modern humans were really different species. They thought that the differences in appearance between Africans and Asians, or between Caucasians and Africans, reflected different evolutionary histories. This theory is usually called polygenism, which means "many beginnings." According to polygenism, each modern race originated from a different ancestral species and evolved apart from the other races.

Polygenism did not stand the test of time. Science rejected the idea when it was established beyond all doubt that in spite of physical differences such as skull shape and skin color, all living humans belong to the same species.

A somewhat different view of modern human origins began to take shape in the 1930s. At that time a scientist named Franz Weidenreich was studying newly discovered fossil skulls of Peking Man. Weidenreich noticed that those ancient skulls had some anatomical features that are also seen in the skulls of modern Chinese people. He theorized that Chinese *Homo erectus* had evolved into the modern people of Asia. Weidenreich then speculated that various populations of *H. erectus* in the Old World, which consists of Africa, Asia, Europe, and Australia, had given rise over time, through intermediate stages of evolution, to all of the modern races of *Homo sapiens*.

Weidenreich claimed that racial groups and subgroups such as the Chinese, Indonesians, Africans, Europeans, and Australian Aborigines had evolved more or less separately, but with enough interbreeding through the ages so that all of them remained within a single species. He thought that the modern people who are native to each region of the Old World are descended from the first humans who lived in that region, hundreds of thousands of years ago.

Starting in the 1980s, some scientists—led by Milford Wolpoff of the University of Michigan and Alan Thorne of the Australian National University—developed Weidenriech's idea into the multiregional model of recent human evolution. Another name for multiregional evolution is the continuity model. Scientists who support this view claim that there has been continuity, or an unbroken connection, between the early humans who formed the first wave of migration from Africa and the people of the modern world.

The multiregional theory says that modern humans evolved through a balance between isolation and unity. As populations of early *Homo* became established in various parts of the Old World, the people living in the core of each region were isolated from the other regions. This isolation resulted in the evolution of certain distinctive physical features within each region, such as Peking Man's high cheekbones and Neanderthal Man's large nose.

And because modern populations evolved from ancient ones, these features are reflected today in the features of modern people, including the high cheekbones of Chinese people and the large noses of Europeans.

At the same time, however, some interbreeding took place among the regions, probably as a result of contact between people who lived near the borders. This interbreeding resulted in gene flow, which is the sharing of genetic material. Gene flow allowed new features that aided survival, such as increased brain size, to spread throughout all regions. While isolation allowed the regional populations of *Homo* to become distinctively different, gene flow kept them from becoming so different that they speciated, or split off

Are today's Chinese people the genetic heirs of ancient Peking Man? Some scientists think so, but others support a different view of modern human origins.

into separate species. Instead, they continued to evolve as a single species.

According to this multiregional model, modern *H. sapiens* evolved over a million years or more, across a broad geographic range that included most of the Old World. A few paleoanthropologists who hold this view think that early humans such as Java Man and the Neanderthals should be regarded not as separate species from our own but as regional varieties, or subspecies, of evolving *H. sapiens*.[14]

The Out-of-Africa Model

Louis Leakey was a British archaeologist and anthropologist who came to East Africa in the mid-twentieth century to look for ancient stone tools. In the years that followed, he and members of his family made important discoveries about early human evolution. (*First Humans* in this series tells the story of these finds.) Leakey was convinced that Africa was not only the birthplace of humankind's earliest ancestors, such as the australopiths, but the birthplace of modern *Homo sapiens* as well.

The idea of an African origin for modern humans gained strength in the 1980s as a result of genetic research (described in the next chapter). That research supported a theory of recent human evolution that has been called the out-of-Africa model. It also may be called the recent African origin or replacement model.

The out-of-Africa model says that after *Homo ergaster* (or *H. erectus*) spread beyond Africa, the humans who remained in Africa continued to evolve. Some of them eventually gave rise to a new species, *Homo sapiens*. In time the ancestral species disappeared, leaving *H. sapiens* as the only human in Africa. Then, within the past hundred thousand years or so, a second wave of migration flowed out of Africa. In this wave, *H. sapiens* left Africa and spread through the Old World, replacing any earlier species of humans that still existed, such as Neanderthal Man.

The strict version of this theory is sometimes called the replacement model because it says that modern *H. sapiens* is descended from only African ancestors. The *H. sapiens* who left Africa replaced the earlier humans in other parts of the Old World. These earlier *Homo* populations became extinct without interbreeding with *H. sapiens*—or, if some interbreeding did occur, it did not result in significant gene flow. Our genome, in other words, contains little if any contribution from *Homo erectus* or the Neanderthals.

What about the variations among human populations, the differences that we recognize as racial or regional characteristics? The out-of-Africa model says that these differences developed within the last hundred thousand years or so, after modern humans left Africa.

As populations of *Homo sapiens* became established in various regions,

Homo erectus was a long-lasting human species that evolved in Africa and then colonized a broad range in Asia. According to one widely held theory, in Africa H. erectus continued to evolve into new species. Eventually one of its descendants—H. sapiens—left Africa and colonized the world.

they evolved distinctive features. Some of these features were adaptations to local conditions. People living in cold northern Eurasia, for example, developed thicker bodies and limbs because this body type is good for conserving warmth. Each region's distinctive features were reinforced by gene flow within the region. In this view, the racial variation we see in modern humans is not rooted in separate evolutionary paths that began hundreds of thousands of years ago. Instead, it is just tens of thousands of years old.

Models in the Middle

Since the 1990s, many scientists have embraced the out-of-Africa model of modern human origins, although multiregionalism also has supporters. Some experts, however, think that the correct answer lies somewhere in between. These scientists have proposed intermediate theories that blend aspects of both models.

One theory is that the key features of modern humans evolved in Africa, as in the out-of-Africa model. These features then spread to other parts of the Old World, not through replacement but through gene flow. As populations in neighboring territories interbred, the new genes combined with old ones to produce *Homo sapiens*. Modern humans did not replace the earlier varieties, in this view. Instead, they assimilated, or absorbed, them.[15] For example, paleontologist and Neanderthal researcher Erik Trinkaus thinks that interbreeding took place between Neanderthals and early modern humans in Europe. The hybrid offspring of these unions had both Neanderthal and modern features. Over the course of many generations, the Neanderthal traits became assimilated into the larger population of modern humans.[16]

Other researchers have suggested that the multiregional model is accurate for some regions and the out-of-Africa model is accurate for others. If this interpretation is correct, early modern humans could have interbred with the descendants of Java Man but replaced the Neanderthals . . . or the other way around. Another theory that has gained ground in recent years is that *H. sapiens* left Africa not once but many times, in multiple waves of migration, and that each new wave of migrants met and mingled with people descended from the earlier migrants. Geneticist Alan Templeton of Washington University in St. Louis has led the research on this model, known as Out of Africa, Again and Again.

Examining the Evidence

The scientific community has not yet accepted any theory as the full and final explanation of how, when, and where *Homo sapiens* came into existence. Although the balance of opinion has tilted toward the out-of-Africa model, paleoanthropologists are still debating the evidence, some of which suggests other possibilities.

Evidence about our origins falls into two categories. One category consists of physical relics from the human past: the fossilized skulls and bones that paleoanthropologists study, as well as artifacts such as stone tools, which are of interest to archaeologists. The other category of evidence is in our genes. To weigh this evidence, molecular biologists analyze the modern human genome for information about how it, and we, evolved. Looking into our DNA, they explore the genetic legacy that we inherited from our distant *Homo sapiens* ancestors.

TWO

Decoding the DNA Record

People have been using genetic science to investigate human origins since the middle of the twentieth century. From early research into the relationship between humans and other primates to the completion of the Human Genome Project and beyond, genetics has become one of our most powerful tools for unraveling evolutionary mysteries. It also continues to raise new questions about the origin of our species.

DNA, Chromosomes, and Genes

The cells of living things contain two types of genetic material: DNA (deoxyribonucleic acid) and RNA (ribonucleic acid). DNA carries information in the form of four kinds of chemical subcodes that scientists have termed G, A, T, and C. This information has two main purposes. First, DNA "builds" each individual organism by coding for proteins. This means that the DNA issues instructions for proteins that will be made from amino acids within the cell. Second, DNA passes the set of instructions from generation to generation. Not only are the instructions copied into each of the organism's own cells, they are copied into the cells of the sperm or eggs that will produce offspring. RNA, also present in each cell, is a chemical that translates the DNA's instructions into protein production.

DNA is a long, two-stranded molecular structure that resembles a ladder twisted into a spiral shape—a shape that scientists often call a double helix. The DNA within each cell is compressed into packets called chromo-

Opposite: *DNA, the long molecular structure shaped like a spiral ladder, defines all organisms, from tiny flatworms to pigs to sheep to us. It is the basic building block of all living things.*

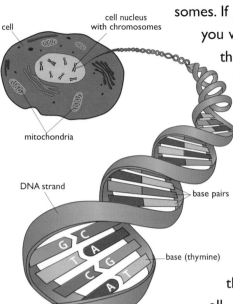

cell

cell nucleus
with chromosomes

mitochondria

DNA strand

base pairs

G C
T A
C G
A T

base (thymine)

Genes are made up of molecules joined together to form base pairs. Long strands of this molecular material, or DNA, are packed into chromosomes inside cell nuclei.

somes. If you could stretch out a chromosome, you would see that the two long strands of the DNA are linked by shorter pieces, like the rungs of the ladder. Each rung, called a nucleotide or base pair, consists of two molecules: either adenosine and thymine (A and T) or guanine and cytosine (G and C). The sequence, or arrangement, of these base pairs makes up the genetic code.

A gene is a sequence of base pairs that codes for a specific protein. Nearly all chromosomes contain thousands of genes.[17] The Human Genome Project estimated that human beings have 3 billion base pairs in 20,000 to 25,000 genes. Only about 2 percent of the total length of human DNA, however, contains genes that code for proteins. The rest is noncoding material, and scientists do not yet fully understand its function.[18]

The complete sequence of base pairs for a species is its genome. Together the genes that fill each place on the genome for a particular individual make up a genotype. Although you share your genome with the entire human race, your genotype is a unique blend of genes from both of your parents, combined to create you. For example, genes in a certain part of the human genome always code for eye color, but it is the specific combination of genetic material inherited from your ancestors that determines whether your eyes are brown or blue. This is why scientists can not only test a DNA sample to find out what species of animal it comes from, but can also use DNA to identify individuals—a fact that has become a key part of modern crime investigation.

Genetics and Human Evolution

Genetic science developed rapidly during the final decades of the twentieth century. Faster and more thorough techniques for analyzing DNA led to new uses for genetic technology, from solving decades-old crimes to screening people for genes that put them at high risk for diseases such as breast cancer. Genetic science also transformed many areas of research in biology, including the study of human evolution.

DNA is extremely useful in evolutionary research because, in a sense, it travels through time and keeps a record of where it has been. Chromosomes split, make copies of themselves, and combine and recombine over generations as parents' DNA mingles in that of their children. As the DNA is passed on, errors in the copying process, or random mutations, occasionally change the DNA. Unless the change is fatal to the organism or prevents the organism from reproducing, it gets passed on, too. As these changes, or variations, accumulate over time, they create what scientists have termed a molecular clock. The clock tells us how long ago the lines of descent leading to two people diverged, or separated, based on the genetic differences between them. If there is not much genetic variation between two individuals, the two lines of descent have not been separated for very long. If there are a lot of genetic differences, the divergence between their lineages took place further in the past.

Through DNA analysis, geneticists can investigate the past histories of large population groups, of individual people, and even of specific genes or groups of genes. There are several different kinds of DNA, and researchers have used them all in the study of human evolution.

Nuclear DNA

The genetic material that forms our chromosomes is called nuclear DNA because it is found inside the nucleus, or enclosed center, of each cell. Nuclear DNA was the subject of the Human Genome Project, which produced a complete map, or sequence, of the *Homo sapiens* genome.

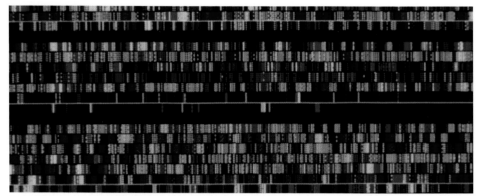

Part of the human gene sequence, as displayed on a computer screen. Each color represents one of DNA's four bases, or chemical codes.

X and Y Chromosomes

The human genome contains two general types of chromosomes. Most are autosomal chromosomes, or autosomes, which have nothing to do with the sex of the individual. The chromosomes that determine whether a person is male or female are called sex chromosomes. The genome has 22 pairs of autosomal chromosomes and 1 pair of sex chromosomes, for a total of 46 chromosomes in 23 pairs. Half of each pair comes from the father and half from the mother.

There are two types of sex chromosomes, X and Y. With few exceptions, individuals with two X chromosomes are female, and those with one X and one Y are male. Everyone, male or female, has just two sex chromosomes, one inherited from each parent. A child always gets an X from the mother, but the father's contribution can be an X or a Y. Whether a person is biologically male or female depends on whether the Y chromosome is present or absent.

Because the DNA of the Y chromosome passes from fathers to sons over the generations, these chromosomes form lines of descent through males. By comparing the Y chromosomes of men from many parts of the world, geneticists have built up a picture of how closely or distantly various human populations are related. One study, for example, found that the Y chromosome of Welsh people, who live in the western part of Great

Britain, is different from the Y chromosome of other British people—but it is surprisingly similar to the Y chromosome of the Basques, people who inhabit the mountainous borderland between France and Spain. Scientists do not yet understand the meaning of this similarity, but it may one day shed light on the source of the Basque ethnic group, a mystery that has long baffled historians.[19]

Mitochondrial DNA

Outside the nucleus of each cell are many small energy-producing structures called mitochondria. They have their own genome, which is copied in each mitochondrion on a special kind of DNA that scientists call mitochondrial DNA, or mtDNA. The mitochondrial genome is much smaller than the nuclear genome—only about 16,000 base pairs compared with 3 billion for nuclear DNA.[20]

Mitochondrial DNA is present in the cells of both men and women, but only women pass it on to their offspring. That's because sperm, the male sex cells, have few mitochondria. When a sperm fertilizes an egg (a female sex cell), the sperm's mitochondria do not enter the egg. Whether the newly fertilized egg develops into a male or a female offspring, all of its mitochondria have come from its mother. Sons inherit their mother's mtDNA but do not pass it on; daughters both inherit it and pass it on. Just as the Y chromosome marks paternal lineages, or lines of descent through fathers and sons, mtDNA is evidence of maternal lineages, or lines of descent through mothers and daughters.

Because mtDNA is relatively short, and because multiple copies of it exist in each cell, mitochondrial DNA is easier to analyze than nuclear DNA (although techniques for

A microscopic mitochondrion contains genetic material called mtDNA.

analyzing nuclear DNA have improved dramatically since the 1990s). Mitochondrial DNA also evolves, or accumulates changes, at a faster rate than nuclear DNA, which makes mtDNA a good source of information about evolution.[21] For these reasons early evolutionary researchers tended to use mtDNA in their studies. And as Rob DeSalle and Ian Tattersall of the American Museum of Natural History have pointed out, "Many of the early studies contained landmark discoveries of the relatedness of human maternal lineages."[22] One such study in the 1980s added fuel to the heated scientific debate over multiregional or African origins for *Homo sapiens*.

The Mitochondrial Mother of Us All?

The controversial study came out of Allan Wilson's evolutionary genetics laboratory at the University of California, Berkeley. Born in New Zealand, Wilson was a molecular biologist. In the 1960s he had helped to show that the chimpanzee and hominin lineages separated around 5 million years ago, much more recently than scientists had thought. By the mid-1980s, Wilson's Berkeley lab had become a center of genetic research into human evolution. There one of his graduate students, Rebecca Cann—with guidance from Wilson and help from another student, Mark Stoneking—worked on a project designed to investigate the origins of modern humans using mtDNA.

As a first step, Cann and her colleagues collected mtDNA samples from 147 people representing a variety of groups from around the world. Then, for each sample, they analyzed a particular haplotype—a set of variations that are inherited together as a unit, even if they involve more than one gene. To ensure that there would be measurable amounts of variation among the samples, the researchers focused on a haplotype in a part of the mtDNA chromosome that is known to mutate fairly rapidly. They found a high level of variation—133 different haplotypes in 147 samples.[23]

The next step was to construct a phylogeny, or evolutionary tree, for the mtDNA. A phylogeny is basically a diagram of how a particular organism, feature, or gene might have evolved. When scientists build a phylogeny, they operate on a principle called parsimony, which says that the simplest way of explaining the facts is most likely to be true. In the case of Cann's study, the facts consisted of a set of highly varied mtDNA haplotypes. The simplest explanation would be to assume that all of the haplotypes were descended from a common ancestor, a woman who had lived at some point in human evolutionary history. The differences among them had arisen over time as a result of mutations.

The researchers' task was to construct a tree that led from that one maternal ancestor to the 147 descendants in the study. The tree would be a set of maternal lineages, or groups that shared a common female ancestor. The samples that had the fewest genetic differences would form groups, the groups that were closest together would form clusters, and so on, through as many levels as necessary. The final tree would show all 147 samples in their evolutionary relationship to one another. In keeping with the principle of parsimony, the phylogeny had to be as simple as possible. In other words, the researchers had to construct a tree that connected the ancestor to the descendants with the fewest possible changes, or mutations.

Sorting and arranging the data was an enormous task, as geneticist Norman A. Johnson explained:

The number of possible phylogenies explodes with the number of samples: three trees are possible with three samples, but over 34 million are possible with ten samples and billions and billions are possible with only 20 samples. Clearly, for anything other than a tiny study, computers must be used. But for a study the size of [Cann's] even an ultra-fast computer could not determine which tree was the shortest (the most parsimonious); thus various methods were developed to aid in the search for the shortest tree. However, back in the 1980s, these techniques were not as powerful as they would later become, nor was computing capacity as great.[24]

Despite the difficulties, Cann and her colleagues succeeded in building a phylogeny for their mtDNA samples. The very first divergence, or split, in the tree led to two branches of descendants in the modern world. One group consisted of people from Africa only. The other consisted of people from every continent, including Africa. The first split, it seemed, had probably taken place in Africa. One branch remained there, while the other eventually spread out across the world.

To create a timetable for their tree, the researchers used a molecular clock based on the rate of mutation in the mtDNA haplotype. They knew from archaeological and fossil evidence that humans first occupied the Asian island of New Guinea about 40,000 years ago. At that point the New Guinean haplotype started its own branch on the tree. Therefore, the amount of mutation that has occurred in New Guinean mtDNA since it formed its own lineage is equal to 40,000 years of mitochondrial evolution. With this benchmark in place, Cann and her colleagues were able to estimate dates for the other divergences.

The most recent common ancestor of all of our mtDNA, they decided, had lived about 200,000 years ago, probably in Africa.[25] Their evolutionary tree also showed that all modern populations other than Africans have inherited mtDNA from more than one lineage. This evidence suggested that early populations of *Homo sapiens* moved about and blended, and that the regions of the world were colonized more than once. For this reason modern people outside Africa represent a combination of multiple genetic legacies, all of them old, but each stemming from a different time and place of origin.

All about Eve

When Cann, Stoneking, and Wilson published the results of their study in the January 1987 issue of the scientific journal *Nature*, the story received a lot of attention. Newspapers and magazines around the world called Cann's theoretical ancestor the "African Eve" or "mitochondrial Eve."

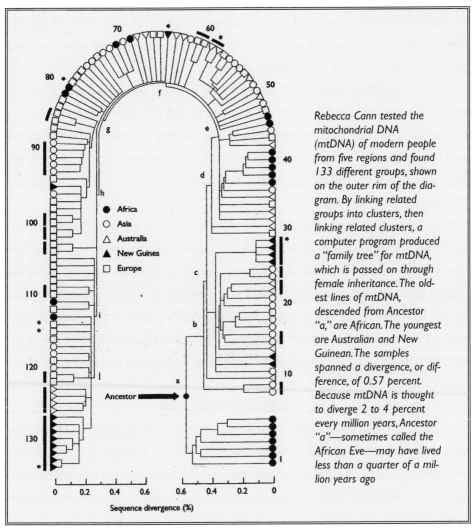

Rebecca Cann tested the mitochondrial DNA (mtDNA) of modern people from five regions and found 133 different groups, shown on the outer rim of the diagram. By linking related groups into clusters, then linking related clusters, a computer program produced a "family tree" for mtDNA, which is passed on through female inheritance. The oldest lines of mtDNA, descended from Ancestor "a," are African. The youngest are Australian and New Guinean. The samples spanned a divergence, or difference, of 0.57 percent. Because mtDNA is thought to diverge 2 to 4 percent every million years, Ancestor "a"—sometimes called the African Eve—may have lived less than a quarter of a million years ago

"Eve" was a reference to the biblical story of Adam and Eve, the first man and woman. It was a catchy nickname for the "mother of all mitochondria," but it created some confusion. Unlike the biblical Eve, the mitochondrial Eve was neither the first woman nor the only woman in the world. When she was alive, other women were alive and having children, too. It is simply an accident of evolutionary history that many mitochondrial lineages have died out, and that the mtDNA lineage of all of the population groups that exist today can be traced back to Eve. If a slightly different combination of populations had survived to the present day or if the same study had been done in the past, before some lineages disappeared, the mitochondrial ancestor would have been someone else.

Cann's mtDNA study gave a huge boost to the out-of-Africa theory of recent human origins. Through news reports and television documentaries, the general public grew increasingly familiar with the idea that the entire world population today is descended from people who lived in Africa less than a quarter of a million years ago, and that those people replaced all earlier human populations.

Among scientists, reactions to the African Eve were mixed. Some saw the study as a confirmation of what they already thought, based on fossil evidence—that modern humans did not descend from Neanderthals or *Homo erectus* but evolved more recently, and in just Africa. Other paleoanthropologists, however, had interpreted the fossil record differently. They thought that modern humans had evolved over a long time, in multiple regions, and in their view the Cann study was not strong enough to disprove this multiregional theory.

Weaknesses did exist in Cann's study. One criticism was that the researchers had used samples from African Americans instead of Africans, and that they had analyzed only a small portion—about 7 percent—of the mitochondrial genome.[26] Critics also questioned the method that had given Cann and her colleagues their molecular timetable. Another significant problem concerned the computer program they had used to assemble the mtDNA data into their evolutionary tree. That program, it turned out, could use the same data to produce thousands of different trees, which meant that the phylogeny Cann and her colleagues had produced was not necessarily correct.[27]

Problems with the first mtDNA study were addressed in follow-up studies by the original researchers and others. As this work proceeded, the results of new studies generally supported the conclusions reached by Cann and her colleagues. One such study was conducted by medical geneticist Max Ingman and others at Uppsala University in Sweden. Ingman and his

colleagues used samples from 53 people from around the world and analyzed the complete mtDNA genome for each. The results, published in
Nature in 2000, showed the mtDNA family tree originating in Africa south
of the Sahara Desert between 120,000 and 220,000 years ago.[28]

The Families of Humankind

In the decades since the mitochondrial Eve first made headlines, scientists
in many countries have used DNA to explore the origins of *Homo sapiens*.
Some have focused on mtDNA, as in Cann's study. Others have used genes
from the Y chromosomes, the X chromosomes, and various other chromosomes in the nuclear DNA, all in an effort to unravel our complicated evolutionary story.

Working with mtDNA, Bryan Sykes of Oxford University in Britain
investigated the genetic ancestry of modern Europeans. He analyzed 6,000
mtDNA samples and found that more than 95 percent of them fell into
seven clusters of haplotypes, or sets of closely related genes, that were very
similar. This suggested that nearly all of the people of European ancestry
who are alive today are descended from seven different women, who in turn
were descended from the mitochondrial Eve. According to the molecular
clock Sykes established for his evolutionary tree, these seven "daughters of
Eve," as he called them, lived at different times, but all of them lived much
more recently than Eve. Sykes dated the origins of the seven clusters, or
clans, to various times between 10,000 and 45,000 years ago.[29]

Mothers were not the only ancestors in the science news at this time.
During the late 1990s, researchers at Stanford University and the University of Arizona mined the Y chromosome for information about father-son
lineages. Their research, published in 2000, identified 116 different haplotypes on the Y chromosomes of their test samples. When they created a
phylogeny for those haplotypes, they found that the Y-chromosome lineages
had shared a common ancestor between 40,000 and 140,000 years ago,
probably in Africa.

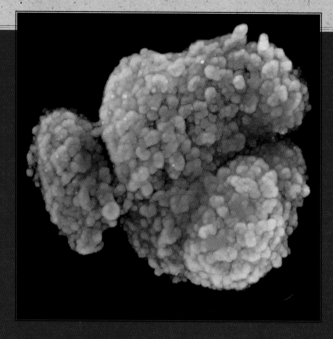

The Disappearing Male Chromosome

The Y chromosome is what makes a male human male. It is small compared with other chromosomes. For example, the other sex chromosome, the X, has 1,000 genes, while the Y chromosome has a mere 27.

It wasn't always this way. Studies of Y chromosomes in other mammals indicate that long ago, the human Y chromosome was probably similar to the X. But somewhere along the line an alteration, or mutation, made the Y chromosome unable to exchange genes with other chromosomes. Because such exchanges counteract the harmful effects of negative mutations, the loss of that ability let negative mutations, or useless DNA—so-called junk DNA—build up in the Y chromosome, which started to lose genes.

Above: *A human Y chromosome. A male human has one Y and one X chromosome.*

"As time goes on this is rotten news for the Y chromosome," say Rob DeSalle and Ian Tattersall of the American Museum of Natural History in their 2008 book *Human Origins: What Bones and Genomes Tell Us about Ourselves.* "[I]f this loss continues, the Y chromosome will eventually be eliminated from the human genome."[89] One researcher has estimated that if the Y chromosome continues to deteriorate at its past rate, it will have all but vanished in another five thousand generations, around 125,000 years from now.[90] Perhaps by then evolution will have created a new way of determining maleness in humans by shifting that function to a different chromosome. If not, the male gender could cease to exist, and the human race, if it is to continue, will have to reproduce by some other means than sex.

Above: *The X chromosome is larger than the Y. A human female has two X chromosomes.*

A 1950 model of a Cro-Magnon Man, one of the early modern humans of Europe

The theoretical male ancestor was promptly dubbed the "Y-chromosome Adam," to go with the mitochondrial Eve—although it is extremely unlikely that the two knew each other or even lived at the same time. Genes that are passed on from generation to generation only through males disappear more quickly than those passed on by females or by both genders, so male lineages tend to be younger than female ones. That's why Adam probably lived more recently than Eve.

Continued study of mtDNA and the Y chromosome led to the identification of more maternal and paternal lineages in our genetic background. Geneticists call these clans haplogroups. Eighteen mtDNA haplogroups and ten Y-chromosome haplogroups, experts now believe, account for the maternal and paternal lineages of all living humans.[30]

Most European and Asian men belong to a Y-chromosome lineage stemming from an ancestor whom scientists call M168. He appears to have lived around 50,000 years ago. A woman whom scientists have labeled L8—the most recent mitochondrial ancestor shared by living Europeans and Asians—lived at about the same time. Scientists think that both M168 and L8 lived in Africa. That's because, although their lineages contain nearly all living Europeans and Asians, they also include some African descendants. This means that the lineages most likely originated in Africa, then spread. The lines of descent from each ancestor split in Africa, with one branch remaining there and the other branch migrating throughout Eurasia.[31]

DNA from Fossils

Most genetic research on the human past takes the present as its starting point. With DNA from the saliva, blood, or tissue of living people, researchers probe into how our species evolved, mated, and migrated thousands, tens of thousands, or even hundreds of thousands of years ago.

Fossils, in contrast, come to us from the past. Hard as stone, often encased in rock, they are the physical remains of not just our long-dead *Homo sapiens* ancestors but also of the human and hominin species that came before them. In a few cases, these petrified bones have yielded up traces of genetic material, letting us examine a Neanderthal's DNA as well as the shape of his skull.

The first recovery of mitochondrial DNA from a Neanderthal fossil was announced in 1997. (*Ice Age Neanderthals* in this series describes this milestone in genetic science.) Within a few years, researchers had obtained mtDNA from other Neanderthal remains and also from the remains of Cro-Magnons, as the modern humans who occupied Europe around 30,000 years ago are called. The next breakthrough came in 2006, with the recovery of Neanderthal nuclear DNA. Researchers are now hoping that in time they will be able to sequence the entire Neanderthal genome. (No DNA has been recovered from hominin remains older than the Neanderthals, and perhaps it never will be. Scientists now believe that DNA cannot survive for more than 60,000 years.[32])

Neanderthal mtDNA proved to be very different from that of modern humans. Evolutionary trees made with Neanderthal and *Homo sapiens* mtDNA suggest that the last common ancestor of the two lineages lived more than half a million years ago, and that the lineages evolved separately after that time.[33]

Although researchers have not found any genetic evidence of interbreeding between modern humans and Neanderthals, they haven't ruled out the possibility that it took place. Only mtDNA and a few small portions of the nuclear DNA have been studied for the Neanderthals. Until scientists can study the full Neanderthal genome, they will not know how it compares with our own. In 2008, however, Italian researchers announced that they had sequenced the entire mtDNA genome from a 28,000-year-old Cro-Magnon fossil found in a cave in southern Italy. The Cro-Magnon genome matched the modern mtDNA genome, and there was no sign of genetic material that might have come from the Neanderthals.[34]

British paleoanthropologist Chris Stringer, a strong supporter of the replacement theory of human evolution, summed up the evidence from Neanderthal DNA this way: "These results match with views, including mine, that the Neandertals were largely or totally replaced rather than absorbed into the Cro-Magnon gene pool, but the samples are small and it is possible that other samples or other genes might tell a different story."[35]

The Genetic Verdict

A lot of genetic evidence appears to support the theory that modern humans originated in Africa and then replaced the earlier human populations in the Old World. Not all scientists agree with this interpretation of the evidence, however, and a few genetic clues point in other directions.

One idea behind Cann's original mtDNA research and many similar projects is that the greatest amount of genetic diversity will be found in the region where *Homo sapiens* have lived the longest. In other words, the population that stretches back continuously to our point of origin has had the most time to accumulate mutations.

Many studies have shown that certain parts of the human genome have more variety in Africa than elsewhere. But what if "greatest genetic diversity" is not a sign of "region of origin" but rather "region with most individuals"? If more humans lived in Africa than in other parts of the world for much of human history, that could result in a high level of genetic diversity among Africans—but it would not necessarily mean that *H. sapiens* evolved in Africa and only in Africa. It might be possible that gene flow from early humans in Asia entered Africa at an early point in the evolution of

Homo sapiens, and then for a long time afterward our species evolved primarily in Africa.

One piece of genetic evidence that favors evolution in Asia came from a study at Oxford University. Researchers examined a tiny section of nuclear DNA: the beta-globin gene, one of a set of genes that code for hemoglobins, substances in the blood that carry oxygen through the body. After analyzing many samples of the gene and constructing an evolutionary tree, the researchers found that modern Asian people have varieties of the beta-globin gene that appear to be about 200,000 years old. These varieties do not occur in modern Africans. The results of this study suggested that at least some Asian traits had evolved in Asia over a long period of time. Beta-globin, in other words, fits the theory of multiregional continuity better than the out-of-Africa replacement model.[36]

Beta-globin also appeared in research that geneticist Alan Templeton published in 2002. Templeton combined the evolutionary trees for ten different segments of human DNA, including beta-globin, two sections of the X chromosome, and the earlier mtDNA and Y-chromosome studies. His results showed that humans migrated out of Africa in at least three major waves.

The first wave was the migration of *Homo erectus* from Africa into Eurasia, which Templeton dated at 1.7 million years ago (although many paleoanthropologists believe, on the basis of fossil evidence, that it happened a bit earlier than that). Templeton's second wave occurred between 840,000 and 420,000 years ago. It involved a different *Homo* species—but not *Homo sapiens*, which had not yet evolved. Finally, *Homo sapiens* spread outward from Africa between 150,000 and 80,000 years ago. Up to this point, Templeton's findings fit the out-of-Africa theory, but he rejected the idea of replacement. He argued that the genetic evidence shows that, rather than replacing earlier humans, each wave of newcomers interbred with the descendants of those who had gone before.[37]

This is the Out of Africa, Again and Again model of recent human evolution. It stresses assimilation, with out-of-Africa migrants absorbing some genes and traits from earlier populations. Templeton's model has received support from paleoanthropologists such as Fred Smith of Northern Illinois University, who had already argued for assimilation based on fossil evidence.

Many scientists now share the view that, in the words of paleoanthropologist Roger Lewin, "Africa has played a dominant role in the history of early modern humans."[38] Although the balance of the genetic evidence does indicate that Africa was the birthplace of *Homo sapiens*, the evolutionary history of our species may be more complicated than the strict extremes of the replacement and continuity theories. *Homo sapiens* appear to have done a lot of moving around, splitting up, and mixing during early human history. Migratory populations could have fragmented into small, isolated groups that encountered one another and interbred after long periods of separate evolution. One lively area of current genetic research, described in chapter six, involves tracing the routes by which *H. sapiens* eventually populated nearly all of the planet, forming the many different population groups of the modern world.

Genetic science has not yet given us a firm and final answer to questions about the origin of our species. As our understanding of DNA grows, and our techniques for studying it improve, our knowledge of our beginnings will no doubt evolve—just as we have done. Genetics labs have produced many of the big recent discoveries about *Homo sapiens*, but our first steps toward understanding our origins came from the fossilized skulls and bones that people discovered in caves and quarries on three continents. Today new fossil finds are still being made around the world, and they remain essential to our search for the source of our species.

THREE

Bones of Our Ancestors

The craggy Carpathian Mountains slice through the center of Romania, a country on the eastern edge of Europe. Steep and forested, home to many of Europe's remaining bears and wolves, the Carpathians became famous as the lair of the fictional vampire Dracula. But these mountains have another claim to fame. They were also the home of some of the first members of our species to live in Europe.

Caverns, holes, and tunnels in the Carpathians attract spelunkers, or cave explorers, from around the world. One chamber discovered by these underground explorers is called Peştera cu Oase, Romanian for "cave with bones." There, in 2002, three Romanian spelunkers found human fossils, including an adult man's lower jawbone and part of an adolescent's face.

Paleoanthropologist Erik Trinkaus, here holding a Neanderthal skull, identified the fossils from Peştera cu Oase as Homo sapiens. He views some other fossils, however, as Neanderthal-H. sapiens hybrids.

After examining the jawbone, known as Oase 1, a scientific team led by Erik Trinkaus announced two conclusions. First, the jawbone belongs to *Homo sapiens*, our species, even though it differs in some ways from modern jawbones. Second, the jawbone is between 34,000 and 36,000 years old.[39] Before Oase 1, the oldest European fossils confirmed to be those of modern humans were about

30,000 years old. That made the Oase 1 jawbone "the oldest definite early modern specimen in Europe," in Trinkaus's words.[40] It is one of many human fossils that paleoanthropologists are using to trace the evolutionary path that led to the people of the present day.

Anatomically Modern

Scientists often apply the phrase "anatomically modern *Homo sapiens*" to fossils like Oase 1—the remains of humans who lived long ago but clearly looked pretty much like us. What makes a human being anatomically modern?

People and the fossils they leave behind can be described in terms of their morphology, which is a scientific term for shape or physical form. Closely related to morphology is anatomy, the internal structures that give an organism its shape. The human fossils that have been found consist only of bones, with no soft structures such as organs or skin. For this reason anatomical descriptions of early humans are concerned with bones—not just individual bones, but also the way they fit together in a skeleton or skull. To say that a human fossil is anatomically modern means that its bony structure matches the bony structure of today's people in ways that scientists have agreed are important.

Skulls of modern humans differ in a number of ways from the skulls of earlier species of *Homo*. Earlier species had large, highly visible brow ridges, which are bulges of bone above the eyes. *Homo sapiens* skulls have no brow ridges, or small ones. And where earlier humans lacked bony projections on their lower jaws to give them a forward-pointing chin, modern humans have definite bony chins that point outward.

On a modern skull, the cranium—the hollow part of the skull that holds the brain—is higher, rounder, and more dome shaped than on earlier kinds of humans. *Homo sapiens'* brain comes in a wide range of sizes, but the typical range is between 1,250 and 1,500 cubic centimeters in volume, larger on average than the brain of any earlier human except Neanderthal Man. The teeth of modern humans are smaller than in the earlier forms, and spaced slightly differently. The modern human face is narrower, too. Finally, the foreheads of earlier humans sloped backward from the brows, and the faces jutted outward past the foreheads. In *H. sapiens*, by contrast, the forehead is higher and more vertical, and the face is flat and tucked in below the forehead.

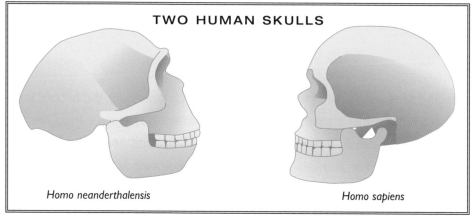

TWO HUMAN SKULLS

Homo neanderthalensis   *Homo sapiens*

Key differences between Neanderthals and modern humans appear in their skulls. The bony ridges above Neanderthals' eyes are missing in modern humans, who have higher, more vertical foreheads. Neanderthals had a bump or "bun" at the rear of their skulls. Modern humans have forward-pointing chins. Although the two species would have looked different, their brain size was about the same.

Below the neck, too, *Homo sapiens* differs from earlier humans. Modern humans are generally taller than most previous species such as *H. erectus* and *H. neanderthalensis*, with longer legs relative to their body size. Our arm, leg, rib, and pelvic bones are less robust, or thick and sturdy, than those of the first humans.

Humans did not become anatomically modern overnight. There was never a time when a *Homo erectus* or *Homo heidelbergensis* mother gave birth to a *Homo sapiens* child. Instead, once the characteristic features of *H. sapiens* started to appear as a result of genetic variation, the species passed through a time of transition. Individuals showed a mingling of old and new features until the new ones dominated and the old ones disappeared.

The transition to fully modern *Homo sapiens* may have taken a hundred thousand years or more, which seems like a long time until you compare it with the millions of years that the hominin line has existed. Scientists have studied fossil remains of humans from many points along the transition, but they do not all agree on just when people became clearly and completely modern. "Modern humans," says a 2007 overview of paleoanthropology, "encompass a very wide range of variation and as such there is no agreement as to what are 'modern' humans, and the date they first appear in the fossil record."[41]

Fleshing Out the Fossil Record

Reading the fossil record is a challenging task. For one thing, the record is full of large holes. Only a small fraction of the hominins that ever lived became fossilized after death, and it is likely that we have found only a small fraction of those fossils. For some of the places and time periods that are especially interesting to paleoanthropologists, few or no fossils have been found.

To make matters worse, most of the fossils that *have* been found are as incomplete as the overall fossil record. Finding a nearly whole skull or skeleton is extremely rare. The great majority of paleoanthropological finds are broken bones, skull fragments, partial jawbones, or single teeth.

Determining the age of fossils is another challenge. Scientists who want to know the age of an organic object—that is, anything that was once alive—can use a technique called radiocarbon dating. Radiocarbon dating tells us how long ago a plant or animal died, but it can be used only on materials younger than about 40,000 years. Another good method for dating ancient materials is to measure the age of certain chemicals that occur in volcanic ash. This method can be used to date very old fossils and stone tools, but only if they happen to be found in or near layers of volcanic ash.

Many other methods of dating fossils exist, but they are not extremely precise. Science writer Carl Zimmer has pointed out that "paleoanthropologists often wind up with estimates that span over 30,000 years."[42] Thirty thousand years one way or the other may not matter to a paleoanthropologist who is studying an australopith that lived 4 million years ago. However, it is a significant fraction of 200,000 years, the span during which modern humans evolved. (See *Origins* in this series for more information on how fossils are formed and how scientists estimate their age.)

Imperfect as it is, the fossil record is an amazing window into the past. Our knowledge of the human family tree is rooted in decades of scientific examination of hundreds of fossil skulls and skeletons. Do these remains support the multiregional theory or the out-of-Africa theory? The answer, unfortunately, is not clear-cut. Scientists have used *Homo sapiens* fossils from various regions of the Old World to argue in favor of both theories or some combination of the two.

Homo sapiens in Eurasia

If the multiregional theory of modern human origins is correct, supporting evidence should be found outside Africa. The fossil record in other parts of the Old World should show continuous evolution from early humans to modern humans, with transitional stages along the way. Fossils from China and Europe, some paleoanthropologists have argued, do show signs of evolution in those regions or of interbreeding between modern humans and earlier species.

China

The oldest-known fossils of fully modern humans found in eastern Asia come from China. Discovered in Liujiang Cave in China's Guanxi Province, they are about 67,000 years old.[43] Supporters of multiregional evolution see these fossils as the end result of a long process of evolution that took place in China. Milford Wolpoff, for example, has argued that the Chinese fossil record, beginning with *Homo erectus* about one million years ago, shows "a smooth transition into the living peoples of East Asia."[44]

Skulls and partial skeletons from several Chinese locations show mixtures of features found in *H. erectus* and *H. sapiens*. Two of the most signifi-

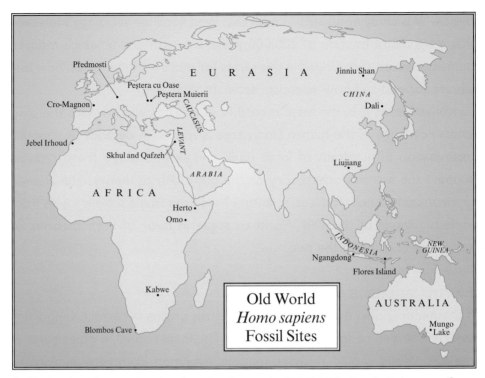

Fossils of ancient Homo sapiens have been found across the Old World. The French site known as Cro-Magnon gave its name to early modern Europeans, while the Czech site Předmostí yielded an enormous collection of early human material that disappeared during World War II. New fossil discoveries—especially in Africa, central Asia, and Australia—may help answer questions about how modern people evolved.

cant are a skull from Dali and a partial skeleton from Jinniu Shan, both dated to about 200,000 years ago. Not all scientists agree, however, that these fossils prove a continuous transition from *H. erectus* to *H. sapiens*. Some experts have identified the Jinniu Shan hominin, for example, as *Homo heidelbergensis*.[45] If this identification is correct, did Heidelberg Man die out in China or evolve there into *H. sapiens*? The fossil record has not yet answered that question.

Teeth have been cited as another piece of evidence for regional evolution in China. Many modern Chinese people share a distinctive feature of the incisors, or front teeth, in their upper jaws. These teeth are "shovel shaped," or slightly curved rather than completely flat. Because this feature also appears in Chinese *H. erectus* fossils, some paleoanthropologists see the shovel-shaped incisor as a sign of continuous evolution from *H. erectus* to modern Chinese people. This kind of tooth, however, also shows up in human fossils from other regions of the Old World, so it cannot be a unique sign of Chinese regional evolution.[46]

These "shovel-shaped" incisors are front teeth that are slightly curved. Such teeth appear in Neanderthal and H. erectus fossils, as well as in some modern Chinese people.

The Chinese fossil record has not yet firmly proven or disproven the multiregional theory of *Homo sapiens'* origins.[47] It has, however, revealed a complicated evolutionary history that we do not yet understand. Discoveries of more fossils from the past 1.5 million years of human life in China may answer lingering questions about the role of ancient *Homo erectus* in the development of modern east Asians.

Europe

One of the most hotly debated questions in paleoanthropology today is, What happened when modern humans of African origin migrated into Europe and encountered Neanderthals? Did *Homo sapiens* replace the Neanderthals or interbreed with them?

Neanderthals were the product of several hundred thousand years of separate evolution in Europe. If our species did interbreed with them, do we carry their ancient evolutionary legacy within us? Or was the Neanderthal line a dead end? The evidence from Neanderthal DNA, so far as it is known, suggests that *H. neanderthalensis* did not contribute to our genome. What about the fossil record?

Neanderthals lived in Europe during the Late Pleistocene epoch, which lasted from about 130,000 to 10,000 years ago. The last-known Neanderthal fossils date from around 27,000 years ago, and paleoanthropologists think that the Neanderthals became extinct around that time. They also think that anatomically modern *Homo sapiens* had begun to colonize Europe by at least 40,000 years ago.[48] Modern humans and Neanderthals, then, overlapped in Europe for some time.

The first early modern human remains to be discovered in Europe were three skulls and some partial skeletons found at Les Eyzies in southwestern France in 1868. These fossils are now known to be about 30,000 years old.[49] They were found inside a rock shelter, which is a term that archaeologists use to describe a shallow cave or a sheltered spot under an overhanging rock wall or outcropping. Because the people of Les Eyzies called that particular rock shelter Cro-Magnon, the early modern people of Europe came to be called Cro-Magnons.

The Les Eyzies remains are clearly *Homo sapiens*, yet some paleoanthropologists argue that these and other Cro-Magnon fossils seem to have traces of Neanderthal anatomy. The Neanderthals had large teeth and jaws, for example, and Cro-Magnon teeth and jaws are often bigger than those of most modern humans (although smaller than those of Neanderthals).

A handful of Cro-Magnon fossils were discovered in 1952 in a Romanian cave called Peştera Muierii, the "cave of the women." In the 2000s paleontologist Erik Trinkaus and other researchers re-examined these remains. Using radiocarbon dating, the researchers found an age for the fossils of 30,000 years.[50] They also noted several anatomical features, such as a bump on the back of the skull and a particular bony ridge in the lower jaw, that are often found on Neanderthal remains but rarely found in modern people. Trinkaus's explanation is that the Peştera Muierii fossils are *Homo sapiens*—but with some Neanderthal added.

The Peştera Muierii fossils and others like them have convinced Trinkaus that early modern humans evolved in Africa and then, when they reached Europe, interbred with Neanderthals. The offspring of these matings were hybrids of *Homo sapiens* and *H. neanderthalensis*. In the tens of thousands of years that followed, the Neanderthal DNA disappeared from the human genome, swamped by DNA from the much more numerous *H. sapiens*. Although we cannot detect a Neanderthal heritage in our DNA, the mixing of Neanderthals and modern humans is "readily apparent" in the fossil record, in Trinkaus's view.[51]

The majority of experts, though, are more cautious about interpreting the fossil evidence. Hybridization is not the only possible explanation for the Neanderthal-like features of some Cro-Magnons. Katerina Harvati of the Max Planck Institute for Evolutionary Anthropology in Germany has called such features "archaic," or very old, meaning that they date back half a million years or more to the last common ancestor that Neanderthals and modern humans shared.[52] Neanderthals and early modern humans may have inherited different sets of archaic features from the same distant ancestor—features that have disappeared from our own lineage over the years.

"We've known for some time that the earliest modern humans in Europe are a funny-looking bunch," says British archaeologist Clive Gamble. "They are a distinctive-looking lot, very heavily built, particularly in the skulls."[53] In the opinion of Gamble and many other scientists, we don't know whether the early modern Europeans were naturally robust and rugged, or whether they got that way through interbreeding with Neanderthals.

Scientists who have compared skulls and skeletons from Neanderthals, early European *Homo sapiens*, and early African *H. sapiens* have found that the *H. sapiens* specimens from Europe and Africa resemble each other more than either group resem-

A cast of a man's skull from Les Eyzies, the first Cro-Magnon site discovered

Facing the Facts

Half of all known Neanderthal and ancient *Homo sapiens* fossils came from kids. That's because, according to Christoph Zollikofer of the University of Zurich in Switzerland, 50 percent of those populations died before they reached maturity.[91] The hard life of early humans took a heavy toll on babies, children, and young adults—or juveniles, as paleoanthropologists call them.

Now the remains of those juvenile humans are helping scientists understand the origins of our species. For eight years Zollikofer and a colleague named Marcia Ponce de León studied Neanderthal remains from many sources, including Gibraltar off the Spanish coast and Uzbekistan in central Asia. They examined sixteen fossils, including eleven juveniles. Then they used a computer-modeling program to project how the young Neanderthals would have developed as they grew older. Finally, the researchers compared the results with models projected from fossils of our own species, *Homo sapiens*, using both recent examples and fossils of ancient humans such as Cro-Magnons.

The researchers found that even from a young age, Neanderthals and *H. sapiens* had distinctive and identifiable features, such as tooth arrangement and face shape. A Neanderthal child and an early *H. sapiens* child would have looked very different from each other. Zollikofer's verdict: "The developmental evidence is quite strong that we have two species."[92] From the fossilized remains of long-dead children comes more evidence that Neanderthals and *H. sapiens* went their separate evolutionary ways and did not interbreed.

Above: Computer programs and model makers turned fossil fragments into the face of a five-year-old Neanderthal.

bles the Neanderthals.[54] This anatomical evidence, on balance, supports the idea of a purely African origin for modern humans. The fossil record does not rule out the possibility of interbreeding, but nothing in the record proves that it took place.

Homo sapiens in Africa

If the out-of-Africa theory is correct, modern humans evolved in Africa. In this case, the African continent should contain the fossil record of our species' evolution: the oldest fossils with *Homo sapiens* traits, followed by transitional fossils marking the shift toward anatomically modern humans, and finally the earliest fossils of completely modern *Homo sapiens*.

Transitions

The first discoveries of ancient humans similar to our own species were made in the nineteenth century, and they came from Europe and Asia. During the twentieth century, however, Africa began yielding up its fossil secrets.

The first find, in 1921, was a cranium from the Broken Hill mine in what is now Kabwe, Zambia. Many paleoanthropologists have placed the Broken Hill skull and similar finds from other locations in the species *Homo heidelbergensis*, thought to be the ancient ancestor of both *Homo neanderthalensis* and *Homo sapiens*. More than 250,000 years old, the Kabwe fossil and others like it are clearly human but not yet *H. sapiens*.

The transition to *Homo sapiens* becomes clearer in a handful of fossils from around 200,000 years ago. Found at Jebel Irhoud in Morocco, near the Omo River in Ethiopia, and at Florisbad in South Africa, these remains span the African continent. They have varying mixtures of archaic and modern features—heavy brow ridges, for example, on high, rounded skulls.

More recent fossils from northern, eastern, and southern Africa show that by about 100,000 years ago, African *Homo sapiens* was fully modern. Scientists wish, however, that they had more evidence of the transition. "Overall, the picture we have of Africa between 300,000 and 130,000 years ago is

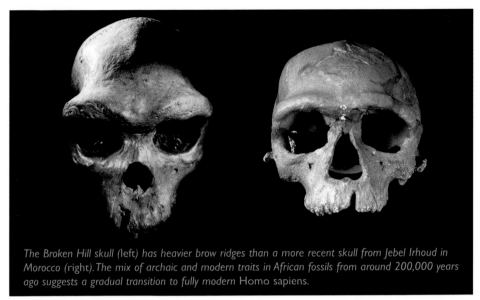

The Broken Hill skull (left) has heavier brow ridges than a more recent skull from Jebel Irhoud in Morocco (right). The mix of archaic and modern traits in African fossils from around 200,000 years ago suggests a gradual transition to fully modern Homo sapiens.

tantalizingly incomplete," say paleoanthropologists Chris Stringer and Peter Andrews. "This is when we believe our species originated, but many parts of the jigsaw are missing."[55] In 1997 a few of those missing jigsaw pieces came to light in an African village called Herto.

Hippos and Humans

Herto is near the Awash River in the eastern African nation of Ethiopia—a region where many important hominin and human fossils have been discovered over the years. In 1997 a team of researchers led by paleoanthropologist Tim White of the University of California, Berkeley, was passing through the village when the scientists saw the fossil skull of a hippopotamus sticking up out of the rain-washed earth. Scattered around it on the ground were ancient stone tools.

When White and his colleagues investigated the site, they discovered more than a hippo's skull protruding from the soil. The recent rains had also exposed the ancient skull of an adult human, trampled by cattle but still recognizable. Later the researchers found a second adult skull, as well as the skull of a six- or seven-year-old child.[56]

Piecing the skull fragments together was no easy task. The child's cranium alone had been broken into more than two hundred pieces. Eventually, though, the researchers managed to assemble the surviving pieces. The Herto skulls proved to be very similar to those of anatomically modern humans, although slightly longer from front to back. In White's view, the Herto specimens represent the point in evolution just before humans became completely anatomically modern. "These specimens are critical because they bridge the gap between the earlier[,] more archaic forms in Africa and the fully modern humans that we see 100,000 years ago," he said.[57]

We know how long ago the Herto people lived because their fossils were sandwiched between two layers of volcanic material that can be dated to 156,000 and 160,000 years ago. With an age of close to 160,000 years, the Herto fossils were hailed as the oldest-known unquestionable remains of *Homo sapiens*. Since that time, however, other scientists have used the same technique to date volcanic material in a sediment layer at Omo, Ethiopia. *Homo sapiens* fossils found there in 1967 were originally thought to be 130,000 years old, but the new tests indicated an age closer to 195,000 years.

The Omo and Herto fossils fit well with the "mitochondrial Eve" research of the 1980s and 1990s, which said that the population of the world today is descended from ancestors who lived in Africa around 200,000 years ago. By showing that *Homo sapiens* existed in that time and place, the brittle, broken skulls of Omo and Herto have provided strong support for the out-of-Africa theory of our species' origin.

The scientific debate about where and when *Homo sapiens* originated, and exactly how we evolved, is sure to continue as researchers dig for new evidence, both in the fossil field and in the genetics lab. Another area of lively debate involves neither bones nor DNA but behavior. What kinds of things does our species do that set us apart from earlier types of humans, and when did we start doing them?

FOUR

The Secrets of Our Success

A whisper of air from behind a pile of fallen rocks caught Jean-Marie Chauvet's attention. The rocks were at the end of a small cave in a rock wall in France. Chauvet and his two friends had found nothing new in the cave, which many people had visited before them. That current of air, though, hinted that the cave might continue beyond the rocks. The three friends dug into the pile and found an opening onto a shaft. All of them were enthusiastic cave explorers, and they knew just what to do. They returned to their cars for a caving ladder, then made their way down the shaft.

At the bottom of the shaft, Chauvet and his friends emerged into a huge, high-ceilinged cavern. It opened into a second chamber where animal bones littered the floor, starkly illuminated by beams from the cavers' lamps. Beyond lay more passages and rooms.

The three explorers probed deep into the cave before starting back to the ladder. On the way out, Éliette Brunel happened to shine her light upward. A small red prehistoric creature, a mammoth, peered down at her from its place on the rock wall. She called out in excitement, "They were here!" As soon as her companions followed her gaze, they knew exactly what she meant. The cave art had been made by the early modern inhabitants of Europe, the Cro-Magnons who lived tens of thousands of years ago.

Chauvet and his friends had made an extraordinary discovery on that winter day in 1994. The cave they had found, now named Chauvet-Pont-d'Arc, contains hundreds of images of the animals that roamed Europe dur-

Opposite: *With manes bristling, ancient horses are frozen in time on a wall at Chauvet-Pont-d'Arc, a French cave that contains Europe's oldest-known artwork. Prehistoric artists created these drawings 33,000 years ago.*

Our ancestors placed their palms against cave walls, then blew powdered ocher, a reddish iron ore, over their hands.

ing the Late Pleistocene epoch: charging horses, lions poised to pounce, a row of marching rhinoceroses, and many more.[58] They were drawn with charcoal and with ocher, a type of earth that contains certain reddish minerals. Among the images were prints of human hands and arrangements of dots and geometric shapes. Similar artwork was already known from caves and rock walls across Europe, chiefly in Spain and France, but Chauvet's proved to be the oldest on the continent. Some of the images were made 33,000 years ago.[59]

The vibrant creations of Cro-Magnon cave artists are now regarded as among the world's great cultural treasures. They are also evidence of a deep change that had taken place in our species. By the time ancient artists brought the walls of Chauvet to brilliant life with strokes of charcoal and ocher, the mind and behavior of *Homo sapiens* had become thoroughly modern, no different from our own.

Symbolic Thinkers

The distinctive feature of modern humans—the thing that sets us apart from other animals and from our extinct relatives—is the way our minds work. Scientists use the term *cognition* to refer to thinking—the process of absorbing information from the world and processing it in our minds. Modern human cognition involves manipulating symbols, as Rob DeSalle and Ian Tattersall explain in *Human Origins: What Bones and Genomes Tell Us about Ourselves:*

> To the best of our knowledge, we human beings are most profoundly set off from the rest of Nature in being symbolic creatures.

Other animals walk on two legs, or have relatively large brains compared with their bodies, have complex vocalizations, or even use
tools; but only we *think* as we do. That is to say, we human beings
mentally represent the material world, and our own experiences,
by discrete symbols—and then remake the world in our minds by
combining and recombining those intangible symbols.[60]

Symbolic thinking means using things to symbolize, or represent,
other things—for example, using charcoal lines on a wall to represent an
animal, a nature spirit, a successful hunt, or the abstract quality of
strength or speed. (No one knows what the Cro-Magnon cave paintings
meant to the people who made them.) It means shaping our plans and
activities with concepts such as past and future, friend and enemy, cause
and effect.

How and when did *Homo sapiens* acquire symbolic thought? We know
that humans did not become modern all at once. Our species became
anatomically modern before it became behaviorally modern. For thousands of years after *Homo sapiens* evolved into a physical form that looked
like us, early modern humans continued to live and act in ways that were
not dramatically different from those of their ancestors, or of the other
human species that still existed at the time.

Because nearly all surviving artifacts of early humans are stone tools,
archaeologists and paleoanthropologists refer to a long period of human
prehistory as the Paleolithic or Stone Age. Early *Homo sapiens* in Africa
and the Neanderthals in Europe evolved during the Middle Paleolithic. At
first, the two species were very similar in terms of artifacts and behavior.
They crafted tools from stone but made little use of other durable materials such as ivory or horn. Although they made several different kinds of
tools, the styles of these implements changed little over the centuries.
People in widely separated geographic locations made the same kinds of
tools, using the same techniques.

Attacking big game such as rhinoceros was risky business for Stone Age hunters. Although early humans slew mammoths, horses, and other large beasts, butchered bones remaining from their meals show that they also feasted on smaller animals.

Middle Paleolithic people hunted game, but they did not fish. They seem to have lived in small groups spread thinly across the land. They wore clothing—at least in cold climates—but did not make art or jewelry. Although they took advantage of caves and rock shelters, they built no structures. (Their ancestors, however, may have done so, at least occasionally. In *Ice Age Neanderthals* in this series, you can read about evidence that pre-Neanderthal people built temporary shelters at Terra Amata, France, around 400,000 years ago.)

Evidence for ritual, ceremonial, or symbolic behavior in the Middle Paleolithic is slim. Neanderthals buried their dead, for example, but claims that they placed flowers or other symbolic objects in the graves are not proven. In the same way, the early *H. sapiens* skulls from Herto have marks

indicating that the flesh was cut away with knives, but we do not know the purpose of the defleshing. It could have been done for ritual purposes, as is the case among some groups today, or it could simply be evidence of cannibalism, which is known from many places and times in history and the fossil record.

Things were different in the Upper Paleolithic or Late Stone Age, which began at least 40,000 years ago and lasted until about 10,000 years ago.[61] The Neanderthals became extinct during this period. Most experts believe that their tools and behavior did not change significantly before their extinction, except in a few cases that may have involved copying artifacts from *Homo sapiens*. But for *H. sapiens*, a flurry of new artifacts and other changes marked the emergence of fully modern behavior and thinking.

Stone tools became more specialized and sophisticated, with regional styles and evidence of frequent new ideas. Archaeologists have identified dozens of separate industries, or sets of tools and techniques, from the Upper Paleolithic. Many of them included a variety of long, slender stone blades. People started using these blades to carve objects from ivory, horn, and bone. They invented new kinds of tools, such as sewing needles, bows and arrows, harpoons, and spear-throwers, or atlatls, which increase the speed and force of a thrown spear.

Upper Paleolithic humans fished. They traded objects over long distances, which suggests an increase in social organization and intergroup communication. They built houses, including large, elaborate structures made of mammoth bones and skins on the grasslands of Eurasia. Art and jewelry became part of people's lives, from small carved ivory figures and heads, to beads sewn onto clothing and headgear, to the panoramas that adorn cave walls. Humans had become innovative, creative, and expressive. They were fully modern in cognition and behavior as well as in anatomy.

SPEAR-THROWER

PALEOLITHIC HARPOONS

Above: *This mammoth once decorated the end of an atlatl, a long-handled tool hunters used to magnify the force of their spear throws.*

Right: *Dating from about 13,000 years ago, these harpoons are carved from tough wood.*

A Great Leap Forward?

Big brains alone, it seems, cannot explain the development of symbolic thought. The brain of *Homo sapiens* reached its present size before modern behavior was common, and other human species had large brains relative to their body size. Neanderthal brains, for example, were as big as ours, sometimes larger. Although the brains of earlier humans may have been physically similar to ours, their minds seem to have been quite different. Mind—the complex interplay of self-awareness, memory, thoughts, and perceptions of other people and of the world—is hard for scientists and philosophers to explain even in our own species, let alone in others. Yet our minds must be different from those of earlier humans, who acted so differently from us. Some researchers think that the key to understanding the modern mind and symbolic thought lies in language.

We know that symbolic thought and language are closely intertwined, but the origin of language is another unsolved puzzle. Scientists cannot say what kind of language, if any, earlier species of humans possessed. It seems likely that some of them communicated among themselves, because they engaged in group activities such as hunting. However, there is no evidence that they had a flexible language that could be used symbolically, to express abstract ideas and to pass knowledge from one generation to the next.

BONE FLUTE

Researchers have put forward many ideas about the origin of human language. Some think that it evolved gradually over a long period of time, starting from a variety of primate sounds and calls, then growing ever more complex as hominin brain size expanded. Others think that full-blown symbolic language emerged fairly recently in human history, perhaps as the result of an evolutionary change to brain anatomy or chemistry. That change created a built-in "struc-

Flutes made from bones appeared in Europe some 35,000 years ago, about the same time as Homo sapiens. *Music in the form of drumming and singing, however, may have been part of human life long before then.*

ture" for syntax, the pattern by which a language translates one person's thoughts into speech that another person can understand. But because words were not preserved until the invention of writing quite recently in human history, we may never know exactly when and how our species acquired the gift of language.

Theories about the origins of modern cognition and language are part of a debate about the shift to modern behavior. Some scientists think that the shift was "an abrupt and dramatic change," in the words of paleoanthropologist Donald Johanson.[62] Jared Diamond of the School of Medicine at the University of California, Los Angeles, has called it "our Great Leap Forward" and dates it to about 50,000 years ago.[63]

Not everyone agrees that humans leaped into modernity. Anthropologists Sally Mcbrearty and Alison Brooks are among those who think that *Homo sapiens* became modern through a gradual process of change. In a 2000 article in the *Journal of Human Evolution*, they argue that the idea of a revolution or leap in cognition and behavior depends too heavily on the sudden appearance of modern humans in Europe, while it gives too little weight to the evidence from Africa.

Mcbrearty and Brooks claim that signs of modern behavior—including bone tools, fishing, long-distance trade, and the creation of art—emerged in various parts of Africa during the Middle Paleolithic, before the so-called Great Leap. One of these artifacts, a 75,000-year-old piece of ocher carved with geometric lines from Blombos Cave in South Africa, may be the oldest-known ornamental or symbolic object in the world.[64] Another researcher who has focused on human development in Africa between 80,000 and 60,000 years ago is John Parkington, an archaeologist at the University of Cape Town in South Africa. Parkington has suggested, based on the mounds of seashells found at many archaeological sites of the period, that humans did make a kind of leap forward when they started eating seafood. The new food source could have provided fatty acids that nourished their brains in new ways.[65]

Is this art? Around 75,000 years ago, someone carved a geometric pattern into this piece of ocher. Found in South Africa, it may be the oldest example of a deliberate creation of art—or it may not. Its meaning will likely always remain a mystery.

No matter when or why it emerged, modern behavior—including symbolic thought, language, and advanced toolmaking—gave humans new advantages in the struggle for survival. Do those advantages explain why *Homo sapiens* is the only species of human alive today?

Scientists do not know whether modern humans drove the Neanderthals into extinction, along with other populations of earlier humans that might have lingered on in Africa and Asia. Perhaps the earlier humans died out because of climate change or some other natural cause. But it is also possible that modern humans, with their superior communication abilities and weapons, outcompeted the earlier groups for resources, or simply fought and killed them.

From australopiths to humans, there were usually multiple species of hominins on Earth at the same time. But by around 25,000 years ago, after the disappearance of the Neanderthals, *Homo sapiens* had spread across much of the world and was the sole surviving species of human. Or was it?

Reconstructed by scientific model makers, Homo floresiensis seems to regard the modern world with alarm. Scientists are still investigating the mystery of the Flores people.

FIVE

An Island Mystery

Modern humans may have shared the world with a completely different kind of human just 13,000 years ago. In one of the most startling and controversial developments in recent paleoanthropology, the bones of tiny humans from an Asian island have added a puzzling chapter to the story of human evolution. Were the hobbit-sized people who once lived on Flores Island the smallest human species that ever lived, or were they merely unusually small members of our own species, *Homo sapiens?*

The Flores find has raised new questions about how and when humans spread through the world. The investigation of the mysterious bones also illustrates science in action, as experts in a dozen fields study the evidence, form and test theories, and debate the results.

On the Trail of Ancient Tools

Flores is part of the Indonesian archipelago, or chain of islands, that sweeps in a vast curve from Southeast Asia toward Australia. Modern humans arrived in Southeast Asia by at least 50,000 years ago. It is not certain when they first reached Flores Island, but the oldest-known traces of *Homo sapiens* on the island date from about 12,000 years ago. If modern people arrived earlier than that, any remains they left have not yet been found. Still, archaeologists did not think that the human record on Flores reached very far into the past.

During the 1950s and 1960s, a priest and amateur archaeologist named Theodor Verhoeven had found stone tools on Flores near the fossilized bones of a dwarf, or pygmy, variety of a now-extinct type of elephant called a stegodont. Verhoeven believed that the tools had been made more than half a million years ago by *Homo erectus* individuals who had traveled to

Flores from a nearby island or from the mainland. Most archaeologists were not convinced. Then, in the 1990s, the tools were tested with new dating techniques and turned out to be as much as 840,000 years old.[66] In 2003 Australian archaeologist Mike Morwood and Indonesian archaeologist Radien Soejono went looking for more tools—and for some sign of the toolmakers.

The search led to Liang Bua Cave. Although excavations had been taking place there since the 1960s, Morwood's team went deeper than previous expeditions. They cut a pit twenty feet (six meters) down through layers of sediment on the cave floor. Their three-month digging season was almost over when they uncovered a piece of bone embedded in the waterlogged bottom of the pit. They carefully brushed the soggy soil from a skull, jaw, pelvis, and set of leg bones.

"At first we thought it was a child, perhaps three years old," Morwood and his colleagues later wrote. "But a closer look showed that the tiny, frag-

Were the tiny people who left skeletons in this cave a new species of human? Or were they simply small, perhaps diseased members of our own species?

ile bones we had just laid bare ... belonged to a full-grown adult just over three feet tall."[67] Signs such as wisdom teeth worn with use revealed that the skeleton, despite its short stature, was an adult. It has generally been identified as female, but some researchers have recently suggested that it may have been male.[68]

The skeleton, known as Liang Bua 1, or LB1, was not a hard, mineralized fossil. Instead, its bones were mushy—"as fragile as wet blotting paper," in the words of the discoverers.[69] To get the bones out of the cave, the archaeologists had to let them dry for several days, encase them in a hardening material, and remove entire blocks of sediment. They also recovered fragments of bone from twelve other humans, all small like LB1, as well as stone tools, charcoal from fires, and the bones of pygmy stegodonts. Cut marks on the bones of these small elephants, made by stone tools, showed that people had butchered them for food.

Paleoanthropology or Pathology?

The Liang Bua bones were taken to Australia, where paleoanthropologist Peter Brown examined them. Brown started with a lower jawbone. "I knew within about 60 seconds of seeing the jawbone that this was something entirely new," he said.[70] The jawbone, in his opinion, was outside the range of variation for Homo sapiens, so there was "no way it could have been a modern human."[71] Measurements of LB1's cranium showed that its brain was about four hundred cubic centimeters in volume, about the size of a chimpanzee's and less than a third the size of a modern human brain.

One immediate question was, How old are these bones? Using radiocarbon dating, geologist Chris Turney of the University of Exeter in England got an age of 18,000 years for LB1. "This was a creature," he said, "who outlasted the Neanderthals in Europe, that was kicking around on the doorsteps of Australia, until at least thirteen, ten thousand years ago."[72] Scientists eventually used a combination of techniques—including luminescence dating, which tells how long ago a layer of sediment was last exposed to sunlight—to date the other bones, which are thought to span a wide range of time. The most recent may be 12,000 years old; the oldest may date to 74,000 years ago.[73]

The Flores find was a scientific sensation. The bones of tiny humans, no bigger than the australopiths that lived in Africa millions of years ago, had turned up in a place where no ancient humans were thought to have lived. Even more puzzling, they were found with evidence of early technology—stone tools and fire—more advanced than anyone had expected such small-brained hominins to possess.

The discoverers decided that the Liang Bua bones represented a new, unknown human species. They gave it the name *Homo floresiensis,* Latin for "Flores Man," although the press soon made the "hobbit" nickname popular. From the start, however, some experts objected to classifying the Flores people as a new species. Teuku Jacob, a leading Indonesian scientist, claimed that the Flores specimens were the bones of an unusually small *Homo sapiens* population. Alan Thorne of the Australian National University described LB1 as "a pathological specimen"—a modern human whose small stature and small brain were caused by pathology, meaning disease or deformity.[74]

Robert Martin, a primate expert at Chicago's Field Museum, has argued that LB1 suffered from microcephaly, a rare condition often caused by a

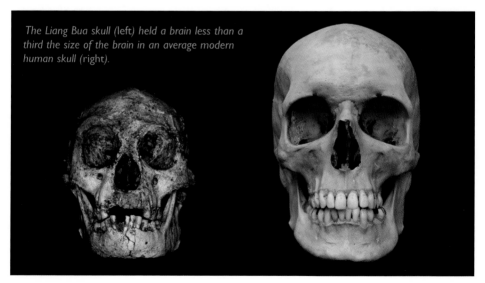

The Liang Bua skull (left) held a brain less than a third the size of the brain in an average modern human skull (right).

genetic disorder. The brains and bodies of microcephalic people do not grow to normal size. Another possible culprit, myxoedematous endemic cretinism, can affect populations that suffer from a shortage of iodine in their diets.[75]

Experts on the other side of the question have found evidence that LB1 is a distinct new species. Three key pieces of evidence are the brain, teeth, and wrist bones. LB1's cranium was too imperfectly preserved for a plaster cast to be made of the brain cavity. Instead, anthropologist Dean Falk of Florida State University used medical scanning instruments to make a computer model of the brain. She and her research team then compared that model with ten modern examples of microcephaly and found that "the microcephalics and the hobbit looked totally different." The shapes and proportions of various parts of LB1's brain were unlike those of the pathological specimens. Falk concluded, "We don't think the hobbit, by any stretch of the imagination, is a microcephalic."[76]

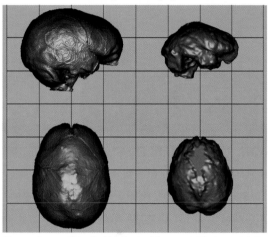

Comparisons of the hobbit brain (above and below right) with a modern human brain (above and below left) revealed that the hobbit's brain was not just smaller but differently shaped.

Anthropologist Shara Bailey of New York University examined two sets of *H. floresiensis* teeth. In her opinion, the small size of the teeth is the result of evolution, not disease—in other words, the hobbits were naturally tiny, not pathological. And according to Matt Tocheri, an expert on primate hands at the Smithsonian Institution, the shape of a small wrist bone called the trapezoid suggests that the anatomy of *H. floresiensis'* hands resembled that of apes and early hominins, not modern humans. The question of whether the little people of Flores belonged to our species might be answered by their DNA, but the bones were found in wet, hot tropical conditions that

Small remains from Palau are those of modern pygmy humans, not members of a different species.

usually destroy DNA. Scientists may prove unable to recover usable genetic material from the remains.

The Flores debate revived in early 2008, when paleontologist Lee Berger of the University of the Witwatersrand in South Africa, along with colleagues from several American universities, announced the discovery of small human remains on the Pacific island of Palau. The little people of Palau were about the size of the hobbits but lived much more recently, just 1,300 to 4,000 years ago. Like the small African people known as pygmies, these remains share key anatomical features—such as the shapes of skulls and teeth—with modern humans. This may mean that *Homo sapiens* can evolve to an unexpectedly small size under some conditions.[77]

First to Leave Africa?

If *Homo floresiensis* is a separate human species, as much of the physical evidence appears to suggest, where did it come from, and how does it fit into the human family tree? Is the hobbit, rather than the Neanderthal, our closest relative?

Some experts think that Flores Man evolved from Java Man, the Indonesian variety of *Homo erectus*. An *H. erectus* population somehow reached the island and then slowly became small because of an evolutionary phenomenon that some researchers call the island effect. This occurs when populations that are isolated on islands become much smaller or larger than populations of the same species elsewhere, because of factors such as limited resources or an absence of predators. On Flores the island effect has worked in both directions. Pygmy elephants lived on the island in prehistoric times, and so did giant rats and large lizards. (The lizards, called Komodo dragons, survive there

The Komodo dragon is a giant island lizard. Did the opposite island effect shrink the people of Flores?

today.) Some scientists think that the island effect could have shrunk humans to hobbit size, but others don't believe that humans with such small brains could have survived as toolmakers and successful hunters.

Another possibility is that both *Homo erectus* and *Homo floresiensis* evolved from a common ancestor far in the past. Some scientists have suggested that the small hominin fossils from Dmanisi in Georgia and the Flores bones represent offshoots of the australopiths. These prehumans might have left Africa several million years ago, before *Homo erectus*, and evolved into new forms as they spread across Asia. This would mean that while Flores Man is related to modern humans, Neanderthals are still our closest relatives. The discovery of additional remains, perhaps in the form of transitional fossils, may one day settle the question.

For now, at least, the origin of the Flores people remains a mystery. So does their fate. Says British paleoanthropologist Chris Stringer, "Here we've got something which may represent that very early stage of human evolution going its own separate evolutionary way, maybe for two million years, so it's a quite incredible story. And it shows that nature, in a sense, was experimenting with how to be human."[78] Meanwhile, beyond the forests and caves of Flores Island, our own species was colonizing the world.

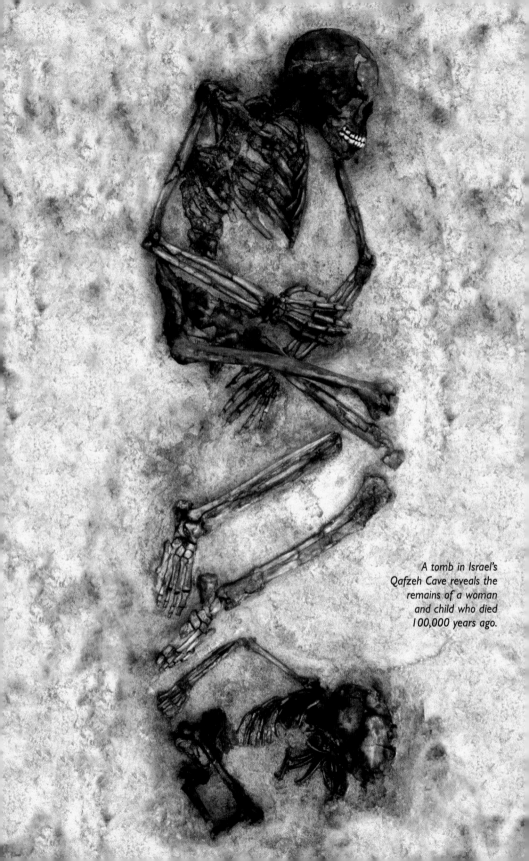

A tomb in Israel's
Qafzeh Cave reveals the
remains of a woman
and child who died
100,000 years ago.

SIX

Peopling the World

A few stone tools, butchered bones, and the fossil remains of several species of *Homo* are proof that humans have inhabited the Levant, or passed through it on the way to Eurasia, for at least 1.5 million years.[79]

The Levant is the name given to the eastern coast of the Mediterranean Sea, a region that includes parts of Israel, Lebanon, Syria, Jordan, Egypt, and Turkey. Traces of very early humans are scarce there, but after about 130,000 years ago, the fossil record improves. Two caves in Israel, called Skhul and Qafzeh, contain the graves of early *Homo sapiens*. Like the skulls from Herto, the fossils of these people were not quite fully modern, but very close. Paleoanthropologists think that they were part of the first migration of our species out of Africa.

These Middle Paleolithic humans from Africa occupied the Levant until about 80,000 years ago. Then they disappeared—no one knows why. We do know that around that time, Neanderthals appeared in the Levant. Perhaps, as the last Ice Age approached, the cooling, drying climate pushed the *H. sapiens* population back into Africa and encouraged the Neanderthals, who were adapted to cold weather, to move south from Europe.

The Neanderthals lingered in the Levant for just 30,000 years or so. They disappeared after *Homo sapiens* returned to the region some 50,000 years ago.[80] By that time our species, now fully modern, had once again ventured out of Africa. This time there would be no turning back.

The Great Migration

Scientists do not agree on the timing of the second migration of our species out of Africa. It may have been under way as early as 80,000 years ago; it had certainly begun by 50,000 years ago.

The migration probably happened over time, as different groups drifted eastward out of Africa. Geneticists think that the total number of people involved was fairly small, perhaps no more than 50,000—possibly even as few as 1,000.[81] They have come to this conclusion based on the amount of genetic variation found among modern-day Africans, which is much higher than the genetic variation in all other population groups together.[82]

The geneticists' reasoning becomes clear if we suppose that the African population of 100,000 years ago had developed one hundred variations of a single gene. Now imagine that most people stayed in Africa, but a few of them left. All one hundred variations, or perhaps ninety-eight of them, were preserved in the people who stayed, but only nine variations were represented in those who left. The result, after thousands of years, would be just what we see today: genetic variation concentrated in Africa.

Into Asia

Researchers have attempted to trace the route of the African migrants by combining archaeological evidence—which is not abundant—with genetic data on the spread and branching of various mtDNA and Y-chromosome lineages. They now think that the route led east from Africa to the Arabian Peninsula. Although a narrow waterway now separates the southwestern corner of Arabia from Africa, a land bridge existed there at various times in the past, when sea levels were lower.

The migrants continued eastward along the coast of Arabia, through India, and on into Southeast Asia. From there, the migration route divided. One branch led southward into Indonesia, Australia, and New Guinea. The other led northward, again probably following the coastline, to China. The fossil evidence shows that Homo sapiens had made their way to China by at least 30,000 years ago, possibly much sooner than that. [83]

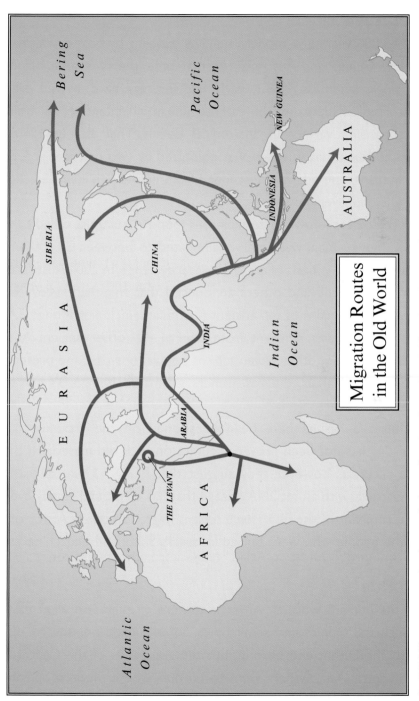

Migration Routes in the Old World

By 150,000 years ago, modern humans had spread south and west through Africa from the place of their origin, possibly in Ethiopia or Kenya. After about 130,000 years ago, some of them migrated north into the Levant, but they vanished from that region after about 50,000 years. Then, between 80,000 and 50,000 years ago, H. sapiens made its second migration out of Africa. Modern people had reached Australia by at least 45,000 years ago. They were in Europe and Siberia 40,000 years ago.

The First Australians

By at least 45,000 years ago, modern humans traveling by boat or raft had reached New Guinea and Australia. (At that time, the two large islands formed a single landmass.)[84] But early humans may have arrived even before that. Fossil evidence of the earliest human inhabitants of Australia shows a surprising variety in anatomical details. That has led some researchers to think that Australia was colonized by two different groups of ancient humans, one possibly descended from Indonesian *Homo erectus*. This theory is unproven, however.

One of the oldest-known fossil skeletons found in Australia, called Lake Mungo 3 or Mungo Man, was traditionally dated to between 30,000 and 45,000 years ago on the basis of archaeological evidence. In 2001 Australian researcher Alan Thorne and others announced that they had recovered mtDNA from the remains of ten ancient Australians, including Mungo 3.[85] Mungo 3's mtDNA was different from that of the other ancient Australians—and also from other *Homo sapiens* populations past and present. Based on genetic analysis, the researchers estimated Mungo 3's age at more than 60,000 years.

The Mungo 3 results have been questioned on the grounds that mtDNA testing has not been proven accurate on such old material. If the results are accurate, however, they suggest that Mungo 3 was an early arrival in Australia, with an mtDNA lineage that has died out. He may even represent a remnant of the first *Homo sapiens* migration out of Africa, offshoots of the people who were buried in Israel's Skhul and Qafzeh caves.

New Worlds

Not all of the humans who left Africa in the era of migration went eastward through the tropics and semitropics. Some turned northward, dispersing into the Levant and beyond into the grasslands of the Caucasus region and central Asia. Others went to Europe, where modern humans were present from 45,000 or 40,000 years ago. Eventually people made their way to the far northeastern corner of Eurasia, the cool forests and tundras of Siberia. Their next migration would carry them into two continents that were empty of humans.

The peopling of the Americas has generated as many theories, disputes, and debates as any topic in archaeology or anthropology. The two main questions have concerned the origins of the Native American people and the date of their arrival.

The first European explorers to reach the shores of the Americas in the late fifteenth century thought that they had sailed to Asia. Very quickly, though, Europeans realized that the lands across the Atlantic Ocean were not Asia but rather a pair of unknown continents, a New World. Euro-

Northern Native Americans go to sea in skin-covered boats called kayaks. Their ancestors may have used similar boats to reach the New World.

peans came up with all sorts of ideas about the Native Americans, suggesting that they were descended from the ancient Egyptians, the Vikings, wandering Hebrew tribes, or even the inhabitants of mythical Atlantis. In a way, the explorers' first thought—that they had reached Asia—had been closer to the truth. Archaeological and genetic evidence indicates that the Americas were colonized by people who migrated from northeastern Asia. They may have come on foot across Beringia (a broad land bridge that linked Siberia to Alaska at times of low sea level), by boat from island to island across the northern edge of the Pacific Ocean, or by both routes.

When did they arrive? For years archaeologists thought that the first inhabitants of the Americas were the Clovis people, named for a type of stone tool first found near Clovis, New Mexico. Based on the dating of sites where these artifacts were discovered, the peopling of the Americas was believed to have started around 13,500 to 12,000 years ago.

By the end of the twentieth century, this theory was losing ground. Archaeological work at sites such as Meadowcroft Rockshelter in Pennsylvania and Monte Verde in Chile suggested that people were widely spread through the Americas by 14,000 years ago. A 2008 article in the journal *Science* summed up the evidence pointing to human arrival in the Americas by 15,000 years ago.[86] Some researchers think that it could have happened much earlier than that, with people migrating south from Beringia by boat along the western coasts of North and South America.

The peopling of the world was completed within the past few thousand years, when seafarers made their way to the islands of Polynesia, Hawaii, and New Zealand. By that time *Homo sapiens* had evolved the range of physical features that we have called racial characteristics. These differences, however, are truly skin-deep. We are all one species, with less genetic diversity in our entire world population than there is in chimpanzees from two different regions in Africa.[87]

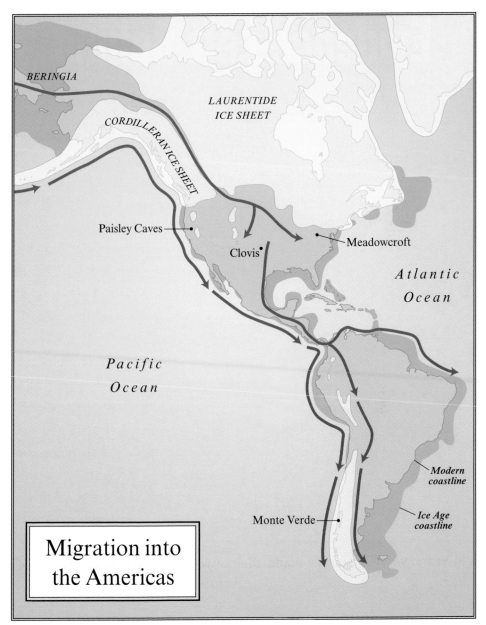

BERINGIA

LAURENTIDE
ICE SHEET

CORDILLERAN ICE SHEET

Paisley Caves

Clovis

Meadowcroft

Atlantic
Ocean

Pacific
Ocean

Modern
coastline

Ice Age
coastline

Monte Verde

Migration into
the Americas

Scientists have long debated the question of when and how the Americas were peopled. Evidence from
sites such as Meadowcroft, Monte Verde, and others has pushed the arrival of humans steadily back in
time. Most experts now think that people from northeastern Asia reached the Americas by at least 15,000
years ago, maybe much earlier. They arrived in multiple waves of migration over time, and they could have
traveled by land between two great ice sheets, by sea along the Pacific coast, or by both routes.

Evidence Left Behind

The humble coprolite can be full of surprises. A coprolite is an archaeologist's name for a piece of fossilized or dried-up human or animal feces—or, to use a less technical term, poop. Scientists studying past human cultures have analyzed coprolites for information about what people ate, what parasites they had, and other aspects of life long ago.

While coprolites are interesting, they aren't usually earthshaking. That's why archaeologist Dennis Jenkins of the University of Oregon did not get very excited when he and his students found some of them in 2002. The archeologists were excavating southern Oregon's Paisley Caves. They found animal bones, stone tools, and more than a dozen coprolites.

Although the fecal remains looked human, only scientific tests could determine their source. In 2006 Eske Willerslev, a Danish DNA researcher at the University of Copenhagen, tested them. He found that six of the coprolites contained human DNA, including certain genes that today are found only in Native Americans.[93]

The next step was to determine the age of the coprolites. Two labs, one in England and one in Florida, performed radiocarbon dating. The results, which were published in the journal *Science* in 2008, surprised everyone. The coprolites were 14,300 years old, which made them the oldest-known human remains in the Americas.[94] The poop from Paisley Caves proved that humans were living in Oregon before the traditional Clovis dates of 13,500 to 12,000 years ago.

Above: *Archaeologist Dennis Jenkins with the oldest-known human remains in the Americas*

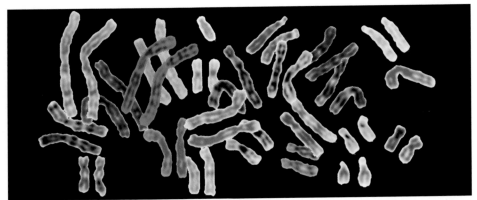

Chromosomes are one key to understanding our evolutionary past. Perhaps we will engineer our evolutionary future by manipulating our own genome.

The Future of Human Evolution

We have learned a lot about the origins of our species, but some of the biggest questions remain unanswered, at least for now. Scientists are not certain exactly how *Homo sapiens* evolved from the humans who came before us, and what kind of relationships—if any—existed between our species and theirs. As we continue to study our distant past, we are also learning more about the process of evolution itself.

A genetic study published in 2007 suggested that evolution has not only measurably affected our species within the past 50,000 years but has actually speeded up.[88] This claim was based on the idea that larger populations provide more opportunity for mutations to occur. The world-wide human population has grown dramatically over the past 50,000 years, and the authors of the study believe that by tracing variations in the human genome, they can show that the number of favorable mutations has risen, and that mutations have spread more rapidly, as the human population has gotten larger. Although these claims have yet to be confirmed, it is reasonable to think that our evolution is still going on, whatever its pace.

Many factors will likely influence the course of our evolution in the future. Some will be natural, such as disease outbreaks; evolution tends to favor organisms that are resistant to disease. Medical science works

Would you transfer your consciousness into a robot or a computer if it meant you could live forever?

against this natural force, to some extent. Medical advances have helped people survive and reproduce, despite illnesses or disabilities that might otherwise be fatal. Technology could play a part, too, in a human-driven evolution involving what might be called "unnatural selection."

Genetic engineering already lets us combine DNA from different species to improve our agricultural crops. We now screen our own DNA for potential health problems. In addition to bringing us medical treatments, genetic engineering may allow us to tinker with our genome, for better or worse. We may one day choose to give ourselves adaptations that will help us survive in new climates or conditions, perhaps on other worlds.

Nonbiological evolution could become possible, too. Some thinkers, such as robotics expert Hans Moravec, have forecast a "transhuman," or beyond human, future. Such a future could come about when humans implant their consciousness into artificial bodies, such as robots or computer networks, or when machines develop the ability to reproduce and improve themselves, evolving into the future without us. Such speculations may never move beyond science fiction. Still, with everything that we have learned from the study of human evolution, two facts stand out. Human beings are part of the natural world . . . and nature never stands still for long.

Modern Discoveries about Our Ancestors

1859 Charles Darwin publishes *On the Origin of Species*, introducing evolution.

1871 Darwin publishes *The Descent of Man*.

1930s Franz Weidenreich develops early version of multiregional theory of recent human evolution.

1987 Rebecca Cann and others publish study that says that the "mitochondrial Eve" lived in Africa.

1997 First Neanderthal DNA recovered; *Homo sapiens* fossils around 160,000 years old found at Herto, Ethiopia.

A mitochondrion containing mtDNA

2000 Swedish study appears to confirm African origin for mitochondrial DNA; Bryan Sykes traces ancestry of Europeans to seven mtDNA lineages; "Y-chromosome Adam" research published.

2001 Genetic study suggests humans reached Australia more than 60,000 years ago.

2002 34,000- to 36,000-year-old jaw bone found in Romania, oldest remains of modern humans in Europe; genetic survey by Alan Templeton reveals multiple waves of human migration from Africa.

Homo erectus

2003 Fossils of smallest-known humans, nicknamed "hobbits," discovered in cave on island of Flores, Indonesia; two projects to map human genome completed; description of Herto fossils published.

2006 Nuclear DNA recovered from Neanderthal fossil; coprolites from Oregon found to be oldest human remains in the Americas at age of 14,300 years.

2008 Mitochondrial DNA genome sequenced from Cro-Magnon fossil.

100,000-year-old remains from Qafzeh Cave, Israel

Geological Time Periods

MYA=MILLIONS OF YEARS AGO   YA=YEARS AGO

EPOCH	GEOLOGICAL AGE	DATES	STONE AGE
Holocene		Present	
Pleistocene	Late Pleistocene	10,000 YA	Upper Paleolithic
			45,000-30,000 YA
		130,000 YA	Middle Paleolithic
	Middle Pleistocene		100,000-300,000 YA
		780,000 YA	Lower Paleolithic
	Early Pleistocene		
Pliocene	Gelasian	1.8 MYA	
		2.6 MYA	

Paleolithic (Stone Age)

Time Line of Human Evolution

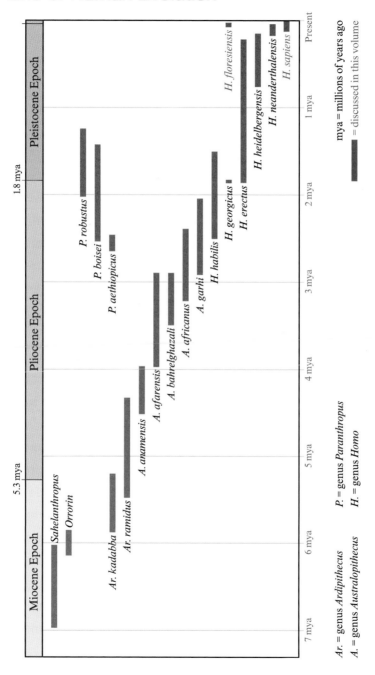

mya = millions of years ago

= discussed in this volume

Ar. = genus *Ardipithecus*   P. = genus *Paranthropus*
A. = genus *Australopithecus*   H. = genus *Homo*

Glossary

adapt To change or develop in ways that aid survival in the environment.

anatomy The physical structure of an organism, especially the internal structure, such as the skeleton.

archaeologist Scientist who studies past cultures, often by excavating ruins and artifacts.

archaic Very old; in biology, used to describe features that remain from an earlier form.

artifact Human-made object, such as a tool, weapon, or artwork.

australopith Member of the genus *Australopithecus* or *Paranthropus*, which includes several species of small-brained, bipedal human ancestors known from African fossils; also called australopithecine.

autosome Chromosome in the genome not involved in determining sex.

chromosome Structure inside a cell that consists of a long strand of DNA; humans have 23 pairs of chromosomes.

DNA Deoxyribonucleic acid, the substance that contains the genetic code or blueprint for each individual and is found inside the cells of living things.

evolution The pattern of change in life-forms over time, as new species, or types of plants and animals, develop from old ones.

fossil Part of a living thing, such as a leaf or bone, that has turned to stone over time as minerals in groundwater replaced organic materials.

genetic Having to do with genes, material made of DNA inside the cells of living organisms. Genes carry information about inherited characteristics from parents to offspring and determine the form of each organism.

genome The complete DNA sequence, or blueprint, for a particular species.

haplotype Sequence of genes that are usually inherited as a group.

hominin Member of the tribe Hominini, which includes living and extinct species in the evolutionary line that split away from apes and eventually led to humans; formerly called hominids.

lineage Line of descent, or evolutionary line.

mammal Warm-blooded animal that gives birth to live young and nurses the young with milk from mammary glands.

mitochondrial DNA Also called mtDNA; a chromosome found in mitochondria, energy-producing structures outside the nucleus of a cell.

molecular clock Any physical feature at the microscopic level (such as a gene) that can be used to measure the time since two species diverged from a shared ancestor; because changes in the feature occur at a somewhat regular rate, the number of differences between the two species equals the time they have evolved separately.

morphology Scientific term for physical form or appearance.

multiregional theory Idea that modern humans evolved separately in different regions from different early human ancestors.

nuclear DNA Chromosomes that contain the genome and are found inside the cell nucleus.

out-of-Africa theory Idea that all modern humans descended from ancestors who lived in Africa fairly recently.

paleoanthropology The study of ancient human life and human origins, mainly through fossils and other physical remains.

phylogeny Study of the ancestor-descendant relationships among organisms; process of categorizing life based on evolutionary links.

primate Member of the order of mammals that includes humans, apes, monkeys, lemurs, and other small animals.

species Group of organisms that share a genome and are reproductively isolated from other organisms.

X chromosome Chromosome in the human genome that is involved in determining sex; individuals with two X chromosomes are female.

Y chromosome Chromosome in the human genome that is involved in determining sex; individuals with one Y and one X chromosome are male.

Further Information

Books

Anderson, Dale. *How Do We Know the Nature of Human Origins: Great Scientific Questions and the Scientists Who Answered Them.* New York: Rosen Publishing Group, 2004.

Fagan, Brian M. *The Great Journey: The Peopling of Ancient America.* Gainesville, FL: University Press of Florida, 2004.

Fleisher, Paul. *Evolution: Great Ideas of Science.* Minneapolis, MN: Lerner Publishing, 2005.

Gamlin, Linda. *Eyewitness: Evolution.* New York: DK Publishing, 2000.

Gardner, Robert. *Human Evolution.* New York: Franklin Watts, 1999.

Goldenberg, Linda. *Little People and a Lost World: An Anthropological Mystery.* Breckenridge, CO: Twenty-First Century Books, 2006.

Lewin, Roger. *Human Evolution: An Illustrated Introduction.* 5th ed. Malden, MA: Blackwell, 2005.

Lockwood, Charles. *The Human Story: Where We Come From and How We Evolved.* New York: Sterling, 2008.

McKie, Robin. *Ape/Man: Adventures in Human Evolution.* London and New York: BBC Books, 2000.

Sloan, Christopher. *The Human Story: Our Evolution from Prehistoric Ancestors to Today.* Washington, DC: National Geographic, 2004.

Walker, Denise. *Inheritance and Evolution.* North Mankato, MN: Smart Apple Media, 2006.

Wells, Spencer. *Deep Ancestry: Inside the Genographic Project.* Washington, DC: National Geographic, 2006.

———. *The Journey of Man: A Genetic Odyssey.* New York: Random House, 2004.

Wood, Bernard. *Human Evolution: A Very Short Introduction.* New York: Oxford University Press, 2006.

Web Sites

http://www.amnh.org/exhibitions/permanent/humanorigins/

The companion site to the new Hall of Human Origins in New York City's American Museum of Natural History offers information about human evolution and video interviews with scientists Ian Tattersall and Rob DeSalle, curators of the exhibit. Pages about *Homo sapiens* include "One Human Species," "What Makes Us Human?", and "The Future of Human Evolution."

https://www3.nationalgeographic.com/genographic/

The National Geographic Society's *Genographic Project* is an attempt to map the past migrations of the human species by analyzing DNA from people around the world. Offerings on the Web site include an interactive atlas of human history, an illustrated introduction to genetics, and a video about the project.

http://www.pbs.org/wgbh/evolution/library/07/index.html
The PBS online *Evolution Library* links to pages on a number of topics, including human evolution. "Evolution of the Mind," for example, is a video interview with Steven Pinker about the evolution of language.

http://anthropology.si.edu/humanorigins/faq/encarta/encarta.htm
The Smithsonian Institution's *Human Origins Program* is an online guide to resources that explain dozens of topics in paleoanthropology and human evolution, from primate origins to the cultural and social evolution of modern humans. The site's "Human Diversity" pages offer an overview of the origins of *Homo sapiens*.

http://evolution.berkeley.edu/evolibrary/home.php
The *Understanding Evolution* site of the University of California, Berkeley, provides excellent explanations of many topics in general evolutionary biology and includes an archive of articles about human evolution, geared for general audiences.

http://www.pbs.org/wgbh/nova/hobbit/
The companion Web site to the 2008 PBS *Nova* episode "Alien from Earth" features articles, interviews, and information about the "hobbits," the controversial skeletons of miniature people found on Flores Island.

http://www.talkorigins.org/faqs/homs/
The *TalkOrigins Archive* links to dozens of articles on the topic of human evolution. The site also contains information about the creationist position against evolution.

http://www.bbc.co.uk/sn/prehistoric_life/human/
The Science and Nature Division of the British Broadcasting Corporation (BBC) maintains this site on *Human Beginnings*, including a section on "The Evolution of Man."

http://www.ornl.gov/sci/techresources/Human_Genome/home.shtml
The U.S. Department of Energy maintains this *Human Genome Project Information* site, a detailed history and description of the international project to sequence and map the human genome.

http://topics.nytimes.com/top/news/national/series/dnaage/index.html
In a series of articles called "The DNA Age," science writer Amy Harmon describes advances in genetic science and how they are changing our lives as well as helping us learn more about our evolutionary past. Originally published in the *New York Times*, the series won the Pulitzer Prize for Explanatory Journalism in 2008.

http://www.asu.edu/clas/iho/index.html

http://www.becominghuman.org/

The Institute of Human Origins (IHO) at Arizona State University maintains these two Web sites. *Becoming Human* includes an interactive video documentary, while the main IHO site features links to current news in the world of paleoanthropology.

http://www.survivingexhibit.org/

Surviving: The Body of Evidence is the online companion to an exhibit about human origins at the University of Pennsylvania Museum of Archaeology and Anthropology. Among other features, the site has biographies of discoverers such as Charles Darwin and Mary Leakey.

http://www.archaeologyinfo.com/evolution.htm

The *Human Ancestry* page of this archaeology-focused site has a virtual "Hall of Skulls," with photos and descriptions of important paleoanthropological fossil finds.

http://www.bbc.co.uk/sn/prehistoric_life/tv_radio/wwcavemen/

Walking with Cavemen, a companion site to a 2003 BBC television series, includes information about human ancestors as well as an interactive "Caveman Challenge."

Selected Bibliography

The author found these works especially helpful when researching this book.

DeSalle, Rob, and Ian Tattersall. *Human Origins: What Bones and Genomes Tell Us about Ourselves.* College Station, TX: Texas A&M University Press, 2008.

Gamble, Clive. *Origins and Revolutions: Human Identity in Earliest Prehistory.* New York: Cambridge University Press, 2007.

Gärdenfors, Peter. *How Homo Became Sapiens: On the Evolution of Thinking.* New York: Oxford University Press, 2006.

Johnson, Norman A. *Darwinian Detectives: Revealing the Natural History of Genes and Genomes.* New York: Oxford University Press, 2007.

Morwood, Mike, and Penny Van Oosterzee. *A New Human: The Startling Discovery and Strange Story of the "Hobbits" of Flores, Indonesia.* New York: Collins, 2007.

Sawyer, G. J., and Viktor Deak, eds. *The Last Human: A Guide to Twenty-Two Species of Extinct Humans.* New Haven, CT: Yale University Press, 2007.

Stringer, Chris, and Peter Andrews. *The Complete World of Human Evolution.* New York: Thames and Hudson, 2005.

Tattersall, Ian. *The Monkey in the Mirror: Essays on the Science of What Makes Us Human.* New York: Harvest, 2003.

Zimmer, Carl. *Smithsonian Intimate Guide to Human Origins.* Toronto: Madison Press, 2005.

Notes

Introduction

1 "International Consortium Completes Human Genome Project," April 14, 2003, press release from International Human Genome Sequencing Consortium, online at http://www.ornl.gov/sci/techresources/Human_Genome/project/50yr/press4_2003.shtml

2 Ibid.

3 "DNA 50th Anniversary," *Nature* 422, April 24, 2003.

4 Jonathan Amos, "Oldest Human Skulls Found," *BBC News,* June 11, 2003, online at http://news.bbc.co.uk/1/hi/sci/tech/2978800.stm

5 G. J. Sawyer and Viktor Deak, eds., *The Last Human: A Guide to Twenty-Two Species of Extinct Humans,* New Haven, CT: Yale University Press, 2007, p. 178.

6 Marta Mirazón Lahr and Robert Foley, "Paleoanthropology: Human Evolution Writ Small," *Nature* 431, October 28, 2004, online at http://www.nature.com/nature/journal/v431/n7012/full/4311043a.html

7 Charles Darwin, *On the Origin of Species,* New York: Avenel, 1979, reprinted from first edition of 1859, p. 435.

8 Ibid., p. 455.

9 Ibid., p. 458.

10 Alexander Pope, *Essay on Man,* Epistle II, line 2, 1733–1734.

11 Rob DeSalle and Ian Tattersall, *Human Origins: What Bones and Genomes Tell Us about Ourselves,* College Station, TX: Texas A&M University Press, 2008, p. 21.

Chapter One

12 Donald Johanson, "Origins of Modern Humans: Multiregional or Out of Africa?", *Action Bioscience,* May 2001, online at http://www.actionbioscience.org/evolution/johanson.html

13 Roger Lewin, *Human Evolution: An Illustrated Introduction,* 5th ed., Malden, MA: Blackwell, 2005, p. 190.

14 Chris Stringer and Peter Andrews, *The Complete World of Human Evolution,* New York: Thames and Hudson, 2005, p. 141.

15 Ibid., p. 143.

16 Erik Trinkaus, "European Early Modern Humans and the Fate of the Neandertals," *Proceedings of the National Academy of Sciences,* April 23, 2007, online at http://www.pnas.org/content/104/18/7367.full

Chapter Two

17 Norman A. Johnson, *Darwinian Detectives: Revealing the Natural History of Genes and Genomes*, New York: Oxford University Press, 2007, p. 198.

18 "From the Genome to the Proteome," *Human Genome Project Information*, online at http://www.ornl.gov/sci/techresources/Human_Genome/project/info.shtml

19 Johnson, *Darwinian Detectives*, p. 100.

20 DeSalle and Tattersall, *Human Origins*, p. 140.

21 Johnson, *Darwinian Detectives*, p. 91.

22 DeSalle and Tattersall, *Human Origins*, p. 145.

23 Johnson, *Darwinian Detectives*, p. 94.

24 Ibid.

25 Johnson, *Darwinian Detectives*, pp. 92–96; DeSalle and Tattersall, *Human Origins*, pp. 145–146; Stringer and Andrews, *Complete World of Human Evolution*, pp. 178–179.

26 David Whitehouse, "Online Study Roots Humans in Africa," *BBC News*, December 6, 2006, online at http://news.bbc.co.uk/1/hi/sci/tech/1058484.stm

27 Stringer and Andrews, *Complete World of Human Evolution*, p. 179.

28 Whitehouse, "Online Study Roots Humans in Africa."

29 Johnson, *Darwinian Detectives*, p. 97.

30 DeSalle and Tattersall, *Human Origins*, p. 150.

31 Johnson, *Darwinian Detectives*, p. 100.

32 Nicholas Wade, "Regenerating a Mammoth for $10 Million," *New York Times*, November 19, 2008, online at http://www.nytimes.com/2008/11/20/science/20mammoth.html?_r=1&th&emc=th&oref=slogin

33 Lewin, *Human Evolution*, p. 186; Stringer and Andrews, *Complete World of Human Evolution*, p. 181.

34 Ewen Calloway, "First Europeans Shunned Neanderthal Sex," *New Scientist*, July 16, 2008, online at http://www.newscientist.com/article/dn14325-first-europeans-shunned-neanderthal-sex.html

35 Hillary Mayell, "Neandertals Not Our Ancestors, DNA Study Says," *National Geographic News*, May 14, 2003, online at http://news.nationalgeographic.com/news/2003/05/0514_030514_neandertalDNA.html

36 Stringer and Andrews, *Complete World of Human Evolution*, p. 177.

37 Hillary Mayell, "Our Species Mated with Other Human Species, Study Says," *National Geographic News*, March 6, 2002, online at http://news.nationalgeographic.com/news/pf/19453033.html; Johnson, *Darwinian Detectives*, p. 101; DeSalle and Tattersall, *Human Origins*, pp. 148–149; "Out of Africa

at Least Three Times," *Athena Review*, vol. 3, no. 2, online at http://www.athenapub.com/outafr3.htm

38 Lewin, *Human Evolution*, p. 206.

Chapter Three

39 Erik Trinkaus and others, "An Early Modern Human from the Peştera cu Oase, Romania," *Proceedings of the National Academy of Sciences*, September 22, 2003, online at http://www.pnas.org/content/100/20/11231.full

40 Ibid.

41 Sawyer and Deak, *Last Human*, p. 224.

42 Carl Zimmer, *Smithsonian Intimate Guide to Human Origins*, Toronto: Madison Press, 2005, p. 111.

43 Sawyer and Deak, *Last Human*, p. 224.

44 Quoted in Lewin, *Human Evolution*, p. 191.

45 Stephen Jay Gould, *The Book of Life: An Illustrated History of the Evolution of Life on Earth*, 2nd ed., New York: Norton, 2001, p. 244.

46 Lewin, *Human Evolution*, p. 192.

47 Ibid., p. 191.

48 DeSalle and Tattersall, *Human Origins*, p. 154.

49 Stringer and Andrews, *Complete World of Human Evolution*, p. 166.

50 "Cave Fossils Are Early Europeans," *BBC News*, October 30, 2006, online at http://news.bbc.co.uk/2/hi/science/nature/6099422.stm

51 Trinkaus, "European Early Modern Humans."

52 "Cave Fossils Are Early Europeans."

53 Ibid.

54 Lewin, *Human Evolution*, p. 196.

55 Stringer and Andrews, *Complete World of Human Evolution*, p. 161.

56 Jonathan Amos, "Oldest Human Skulls Found," *BBC News*, June 11, 2003, online at http://news.bbc.co.uk/1/hi/sci/tech/2978800.stm

57 Ibid.

Chapter Four

58 "The Cave of Chauvet-Pont-d'Arc," online at http://www.culture.gouv.fr/culture/arcnat/chauvet/en/

59 DeSalle and Tattersall, *Human Origins*, p. 194.

60 Ibid., p. 191.

61 Stringer and Andrews, *Complete World of Human Evolution*, p. 210.

62 Johanson, "Origins of Modern Humans."

63 Jared Diamond, *Guns, Germs, and Steel: The Fates of Human Societies*, New York: Norton, 1999, paperback ed., p. 39.

64 Sally Mcbrearty and Alison Brooks, "The Revolution That Wasn't: A New Interpretation of the Origin of Modern Human Behavior," *Journal of Human Evolution*, vol. 39, issue 5, November 2000, pp. 523–524, online at http://www.hss.caltech.edu/~steve/files/mcbrearty.pdf; DeSalle and Tattersall, *Human Origins*, p. 198.

65 Guy Gugliotta, "The Great Human Migration," *Smithsonian*, July 2008, p. 63.

Chapter Five

66 Sawyer and Deak, *Last Human*, p. 178; Mike Morwood, Thomas Sutinka, and Richard Roberts, "The People Time Forgot: Flores Find," *National Geographic News*, April 2005, online at http://ngm.nationalgeographic.com/print/features/world/asia/georgia/flores-hominids-text

67 Morwood and others, "The People Time Forgot."

68 "Alien from Earth," PBS *Nova*, online at http://www.pbs.org/wgbh/nova/hobbit/brains.html

69 Morwood and others, "The People Time Forgot."

70 Quoted in Morwood and others, "The People Time Forgot."

71 Peter Brown, in "Alien from Earth," PBS *Nova*, online at http://www.pbs.org/wgbh/nova/hobbit/program.html

72 Chris Turney, in "Alien from Earth."

73 Sawyer and Deak, *Last Human*, p.178.

74 Alan Thorne, in "Alien from Earth."

75 Colin Barras, "Were the Hobbits Cretins?" *New Scientist*, March 5, 2008, online at http://www.newscientist.com/blog/shortsharpscience/2008/03/were-hobbits-cretins.html

76 Dean Falk, in "Alien from Earth."

77 "Micronesian Islands Colonized by Small-Bodied Humans," *Science Daily*, March 11, 2008, online at http://www.sciencedaily.com/releases/2008/03/080310151958.htm

78 Chris Stringer, in "Alien from Earth."

Chapter Six

79 Stringer and Andrews, *Complete World of Human Evolution*, p. 162.

80 Zimmer, *Smithsonian Intimate Guide to Human Origins*, p. 127.

81 Gugliotta, "Great Human Migration," p. 63.

82 Zimmer, *Smithsonian Intimate Guide to Human Origins*, p. 128.

83 Stringer and Andrews, *Complete World of Human Evolution*, p. 195.

84 Gugliotta, "Great Human Migration," p. 64.

85 Gregory Adcock, Alan Thorne, and others, "Mitochondrial DNA Sequences in Ancient Australians: Implications for Modern Human Origins," *Proceedings of the National Academy of Sciences*, vol. 98, no. 2, January 16, 2001, online at http://www.pnas.org/content/98/2/537.full

86 Ted Goebel and others, "The Late Pleistocene Dispersal of Modern Humans in the Americas," *Science*, vol. 319, no. 5869, March 14, 2008, pp. 1497–1502.

87 Maggie Fox, "Chimps More Diverse than Humans," *ABC Science*, April 23, 2007, online at http://www.abc.net.au/science/articles/2007/04/23/1904301.htm

88 John Hawks, Henry Harpending, and others, "Recent Acceleration of Human Adaptive Evolution," *Proceedings of the National Academy of Sciences*, vol. 104, no. 52, December 26, 2007, pp. 20753–20758.

Sidebars

89 DeSalle and Tattersall, *Human Origins*, p. 140.

90 Ibid.

91 Ben Harder, "Telltale Face Betrays Neandertals as Non-Human," *National Geographic News*, August 2, 2001, online at http://news.nationalgeographic.com/news/2001/08/0802_neandertal.html

92 Ibid.

93 Andrew Curry, "Pre-Clovis Breakthrough," *Archaeology*, April 3, 2008, online at http://www.archaeology.org/online/features/coprolites/

94 Ibid.

Index

**Page numbers for illustrations
are in boldface**

About the Author

REBECCA STEFOFF has written many books about natural history and evolution for young adults, including *Chimpanzees* (2004) and *The Primate Order* (2006), both published by Benchmark Books. *The Primate Order* was one of twelve books that she wrote for the FAMILY TREES series, which explored topics in evolutionary science and biology. Stefoff also wrote about evolutionary science in *Charles Darwin and the Evolution Revolution* (1996, Oxford University Press), after which she appeared in the A&E *Biography* program on Darwin and his work. Information about Stefoff and her books for young people is available online at www.rebeccastefoff.com.